# New Times in the Old South

*Also by Maryln Schwartz*

A Southern Belle Primer
(Or Why Princess Margaret Will Never Be a Kappa Kappa Gamma)

# New Times in the Old South

## Or Why Scarlett's in Therapy and Tara's Going Condo

By

Maryln Schwartz

Harmony Books
New York

Published by Harmony Books, a division of Crown Publishers, Inc., 201 East 50th Street, New York, New York 10022.
Member of the Crown Publishing Group.

Random House, Inc. New York, Toronto, London, Sydney, Auckland

Harmony and colophon are trademarks of Crown Publishers, Inc.

Manufactured in the United States of America

Library of Congress Cataloging-in-Publication Data
Schwartz, Maryln.
New times in the old south, or Why Scarlett's in therapy and Tara's going condo / by Maryln Scwartz.—
1st ed.
1. Southern States—Social life and customs—1865- —Humor.
2. Women—Southern States—Social life and customs—Humor.
I. Title. II. Title: Why Scarlett's in therapy and Tara's going condo.
F216.2.S4 1993
975'.04—dc20
93-19268 CIP

ISBN 0-517-59553-2

10 9 8 7 6 5 4 3 2 1
First Edition

To my sister,

Marsha

# Acknowledgments

Very special thanks to my wonderful editor, Shaye Areheart, who hasn't forgotten she's a New South woman, even in New York City. And to my wonderful agent, Joy Harris, a New York City lady who's surely got a Southern soul.

And of course to my many new and old friends who helped me throughout this book and made me realize once more why the South has always been such a lovely place to live. I'd mention you all by name, but I've been told by an Old South lady who knows, that to mistakenly leave someone out of an acknowledgment is worse than forgetting to write a thank-you note.

# $\mathscr{A}$uthor's Note

People are constantly asking what constitutes the South. Is Texas too Southwestern? Is Virginia too East Coast? Traditionally, the South is defined by the states that seceded from the Union during the Civil War— Texas, Arkansas, Louisiana, Tennessee, Mississippi, Alabama, Georgia, Florida, South Carolina, North Carolina and Virginia, as well as Kentucky as a border state.

But there is an easier way of deciding. Just go into any "home cooking" restaurant in any town you're visiting. If the menu lists macaroni and cheese as a vegetable—you know you're in the South.

# Contents

# Introduction

The South has always had a *mystique*—moonlight, magnolias and Scarlett tantalizing the Tarleton twins at the Twelve Oaks barbecue. Of course there was war, there was adversity, there was Rhett not giving a damn anymore. But somehow we knew there would always be a Tara and Scarlett would always endure.

And she has. But just as there's a New South, there's also a new Scarlett.

Sure, she still turns to Tara in times of tribulation. But in the New South, there's lots more Taras to turn to—the Tara Curl Up and Dye Beauty Emporium with a manicure sculptress in residence six days a week; the Tara Good-Eats Barbecue Buffet featuring nouvelle

*There are New South Taras, Scarletts and Twelve Oaks all over Georgia.* © Chris Sullivan

grits with raspberry butter; and the Tara Arms condos with half-price mint juleps every Thursday night at the clubhouse bar.

But the South is still the South, so don't think the old ways have gone away completely. Scarlett still clings to tradition, worships her daddy and likes to dress up and flirt. Only now she's in group therapy to help her understand why.

And in the New South, mothers are finding that their daughters are more apt to sport Gucci briefcases than they are to wear white gloves. And some of those same daughters are opting to be in the commodities market rather than the debutante cotillion, which means—much to the horror of Southern grandmothers—that some Northern girl is now chairing the Magnolia Charity Ball.

Of course, when times seem too different and the old ways too far

away, the 1990s Scarlett can still feel taken care of by running down the road to Twelve Oaks. Only now it's called the Twelve Oaks Auto Body Repair Shop and Ashley has sold out to a guy named Bubba who accepts Visa, MasterCard and American Express.

There are certainly many changes in the New South. There's also a lot of new energy and new excitement. But just like in the Old South, there is some misunderstanding. When Moses came down from Mt. Sinai

there was no eleventh commandment that said, "Thou Shalt Not Live Below Teaneck, N.J." But some people from up North just don't believe it.

When Bill Clinton and Al Gore were nominated as candidates for President and Vice President of the United States, national newspapers and magazines immediately came up with stories and charts promising to "help understand the Southern man."

Southerners were amused. Four years before, no one had written helpful hints on "how to explain the Eastern

man"—even though that certainly would have helped Michael Dukakis.

Today Bill and Al are firmly ensconced in the White House and a lot of people are finding themselves playing catch-up.

"Oh my God," said one Washington insider, "did you ever think we'd be name-dropping Arkansas?"

But despite all the sudden national attention, people from "other places" still aren't quite sure what to make of the South.

A fourth-generation Chattanooga man says he keeps trying to tell his Pennsylvania relatives that there are just as many people named William Robert in Tennessee as there are people named Billy Bob.

"But they just don't believe me," he explains. His lament has practically become the Southern national anthem.

"Just because we talk slow doesn't mean we think slow," others point out. On the East Coast they seem to think there's something funny about riding around in a pickup truck. Well in the Deep South, we don't think it's all that natural to hurdle through the dark in a crowded subway.

It's the women of the South who feel the greatest need to look at all this with a sense of humor, but it doesn't help when these belles have to keep explaining that the size of one's hairdo has never been directly disproportionate to the size of one's IQ.

Of course, Southerners are patient. They're getting a big kick out of seeing how long it takes all these newcomers to start wearing pale pink in the dead of winter and cowboy boots all year round.

But still, there are a lot of people sitting in restaurants in New York eating polenta and turning up their noses

at all those restaurants in Georgia that serve grits. What they don't understand is these dishes are practically the same thing. Okay, to be fair, there is one major difference.

About $15 an entrée.

Chapter One

# Who *Are* Those People?

I know it's good for us that all these new people are moving here. It's fine that they're helping build the new symphony halls and helping fund the new hospital drives. It's just that they don't do things like we've always done them. They have daughters who are getting married in places like Jackson and Mobile and putting *Tupperware* on their bridal registries. Dear Lord! Whatever happened to Spode and Wedgwood? I'm just glad Mama didn't live to see it.

—A woman from the Mississippi Delta commenting on changing times in the South

## an You Believe It?

This is the New South—new times, new people, new money. Bubba's getting his master's degree. Sister's in the statehouse. And grandmother is turning over in her grave.

These are exciting times. These are frustrating times. There's so much to digest.

British rock stars are moving to Atlanta. The mayor of Savannah is a woman from New Jersey. And new people—*people no one has ever heard of!*—are spending money like water in Dallas.

"You want to know the New South, I'll tell you the New South," says one grande dame from Tennessee. "When I was growing up, my mother wouldn't even let me mention Elvis Presley's name in our house. Now the Memphis Junior League has practically dedicated their cookbook to him."

Of course, this is a particularly tough time for this old-line belle to examine these new goings-on. As she will tell you, things are hitting too close to home. Her son has fallen in love with a very *untraditional* Southern girl.

"She's from a lovely family," the potential mother-in-law laments. "But this darling, charming girl *is in the Merchant Marines!*"

Her son keeps telling her this is a terrific thing for a woman to do. The girlfriend is on the cutting edge of maritime technology. When she gets out of the service her options for a high-paying job will be greatly enhanced.

But the mother just isn't ready for this. She keeps trying to decide where this nice Southern girl got off-track.

"She's very bright, but she went to a college that didn't have sororities," the Old South belle explains. "That makes a difference. The emphasis was entirely different. I don't know of *any* sorority girls who have joined the Merchant Marines."

But it's a bold belle from Montgomery who has really defined the New South. She's named her daughter Rhett.

"It's right for the times," Linda Gail Rogers explains. "I want my daughter to be Southern—but with an attitude. Rhett's a power name with lots of old tradition. I was raised to try to be Miss Alabama. I'm raising my daughter to be *governor* of Alabama."

But even in the midst of a legislative crisis, it never hurts to have a good hairdo, so Linda Gail is still making sure her daughter has the traditional dancing and posture lessons. After all, the spotlight is still the spotlight—it's just the arena that's different.

Governor Ann Richards is the perfect New South woman. She's strong, she's smart, she's effective. And when she went to New York to chair the 1992 Democratic National Convention, she took along her hairdresser.

Yet the governor is in no way a frivolous woman. She's a sharp dresser who has little time to spend making herself look good. She is keenly aware of the role women are playing in politics in the New South. Even in macho Texas, every big city has had a woman as mayor, which prompts Governor Richards to frequently point out, "This is Texas, where men are men and women are mayors."

The governor's lacquered, never-out-of-place white hair has become her trademark. On *her* inaugural day, she marched in a parade to the steps of the state capitol.

Friends and supporters walked along with her, waving signs and banners. One man, however, went even further in his tribute. He came dressed as a can of hairspray.

Southern women have always excelled in beauty

**Texas Monthly**

*JULY 1992 • $2.50*

## WHITE HOT MAMA

Ann Richards Is Riding High. Can She Be the First Woman President?

pageants, but now they are beginning to do just as well in the political arena. In Jonesboro, Arkansas, Blanche Lambert, a former receptionist to Democratic Congressman Bill Alexander, decided to challenge her old boss for his congressional seat.

"Now here's the shocking part," says one Jonesboro maven. "She *won*. Everyone says the reason she won is her old boss had a good-old-boy mentality and didn't think that some Southern lady could ever beat him. That was his downfall.

"That and the fact that he bounced checks and didn't bother to show up to vote for the Clean Air Act but did show up to vote for a $30,000 pay raise."

The former receptionist is now a freshman member of Congress.

Of course, one of the most important differences in the New South is all the new people. East Coast and

*Texas Monthly chose to portray Governor Ann Richards as this very New South woman. They used a body double. The governor loved the outfit.*

© *Texas Monthly*, Jim Myers

West Coast companies are relocating here and, along with all the new jobs and new money, they're bringing in thousands of employees with new ideas.

Go to a party in Houston and you're likely to run into anyone from Mrs. Anwar Sadat's gynecologist to the former President of the United States, who was once a *real* Connecticut Yankee.

But it's places like Atlanta that're really attracting the glitzy newcomers. Entertainers Elton John and Sting live in Atlanta at least part of the year. Former Russian gymnast Olga Korbut now makes Georgia her home, and of course, actress Jane Fonda and CNN founder Ted Turner spend a lot of time on their plantation not far from Atlanta.

Some folks weren't sure how Atlanta would take to Jane because of her radical antiwar stand during the Vietnam War. (This was never a popular stand in the Deep South.)

But as it turns out, it wasn't politics that set Atlanta tongues wagging.

This is the New South. Atlanta has political diversity just like everywhere else. So a former radical who's led millions of Americans to a fitter, healthier lifestyle can be forgiven a youthful mistake or two. No, it was a *fashion* statement that caused talk this time.

The actress wore a *black* dress to her stepdaughter's wedding, still a *real* Southern no-no. One society writer was even moved to take up this issue in print.

"I think it was good for Jane to hear that," says one Atlanta woman. "We don't expect her to follow Southern rules because she isn't Southern. And besides, there are no *real* rules anymore. But still, black just isn't appropriate for that kind of occasion. It might do in places like New York or L.A., but not in Atlanta. Atlanta is a jewel-tone town."

# Those Second Wives Are Marching Through, Like Sherman to the Sea!

"The sociologists will tell you that money historically changed the Old South," one Alabama woman explains. "But I'll tell you the real reason. It's not the economics, it's not the modern-day technology, it's not the new people moving here from up north. It's those *second wives*. They're coming in and changing everything so their husbands won't be reminded of their first marriages.

"Back when I was a young woman you didn't have this problem. Southern women didn't get divorced. Only hussies got divorced. Now it's happening everywhere you turn."

Women all over the South agree. They say divorce is particularly felt in Southern society, where it's breaking up some of the oldest of the old guard Southern tradition. It's also causing clubs all over the South to change their rules.

Old-line Southern country clubs have always been pretty much total male bastions. Women were members through their fathers or husbands. Single women with clout might become *associate* members, but they couldn't vote. If a man's membership was inherited by his daughter, it was put in the son-in-law's name. Not a problem in the old days. But divorce became so prevalent, the sons-in-law were keeping memberships and bringing in their *new* wives.

"The money was being watered down and the clout was going out of the family," explained one member of an old-line Georgia club. "Something had to be done. Our sisters, our cousins and, in some instances, our mothers were being replaced by people we had never heard of."

As a result, the clubs are now allowing women to be members and daughters to inherit memberships.

Even if tradition is being preserved on the one hand, a lot of Old South men are not happy with the change.

"It's a breaking down of rules," one male member of the River Oaks Country Club in Houston told a friend. "I don't care if my daughter can be a member of the club. I just hate the breaking down of rules. It's never the same when that happens."

But the effects of change, like those of divorce, go far beyond the country club. In small towns, it can be particularly brutal—especially in places where social clubs are almost the only entertainment in town.

The old friends are loyal and don't invite the new wife to join the organization that embraces the first wife. So the new wives have to make their own marks and have formed new groups, new projects and new alliances.

In some places, there are unwritten rules to make these transitions less difficult.

"For instance," says one, "the first wife usually gets the Junior League. The new wife gets the Best-Dressed List. But there are so many new wives and so many new social endeavors that we've changed our whole social structure. It gets very complicated. And some of these new wives are coming from places like California and Indiana and they aren't as dedicated to the old ways."

"I spent years belonging to groups that would advance my husband socially," says another woman. "He said that's what he wanted. Now his new wife doesn't do a thing to help his career. She's joining clubs to help her own business interest. She doesn't volunteer, she networks. There's no problem about whether to have two Mrs. James Johnsons with recipes in the Junior League cookbook. She has no recipes. She doesn't cook."

But some things never change. In Charleston, the St. Cecelia's Ball committee has not altered their rules to accommodate new situations. Only men are members and a woman can only come to the annual event with her father or her husband. If a woman divorces her first husband and marries another man who is also a member, she still cannot attend. There is a firm rule that *no* divorced woman may attend the St. Cecelia's Ball.

Charleston women have always found this rule to be outrageous.

"Of course all us divorced women will soon have the last laugh," says one. "There's hardly anybody left who hasn't been divorced at least once. Give them a year or two and there won't be anyone left that they can invite."

Others will also tell you to just be patient. It's the second wives who have the greatest struggles. The third wives fare much better.

"That's right, honey," says one multi-married belle. "It's much easier to follow the bitch than it is to follow the saint."

## The New Partnerships

Even the traditional wife who stays at home and does not work is changing her role in the New South. When Hillary Clinton moved into the west wing of the White House, it was more than just a bold new experience for a Southern couple. These new partnerships are happening everywhere in the South—from the political arenas to the boardrooms.

The eight-year marriage of Bob and Elyse Lanier of Houston has gone a bit further than just being together in sickness and in health. He was a widower when she became his wife. They decided their marriage would be a very modern one, a partnership in every sense of the word.

Mrs. Lanier says they are never apart. And she means *never*. She even moved with her husband into the Houston mayor's office. It was the talk of the town for months.

In 1992, after his swearing in, Mrs. Lanier brought in a decorator to spruce up her husband's third-floor working space. And while he was at it, the decorator also helped renovate an adjoining storage area to be used as her City Hall quarters.

Mrs. Lanier attends some meetings, watches videotapes of others and plans her own agenda to better promote Houston.

Her supporters say she is doing nothing more for her husband than other political wives have always done. But Mrs. Lanier is a glamorous brunette who wears good jewelry and is always pictured with her husband. She has become so high-profile that outsiders are questioning who runs the show.

The First Lady says she has been hurt by such charges. She's not interested in running the police or fire departments, she just wants to be as near as possible, to see that her husband is comfortable and happy.

Since he's always so happy when he's involved in politics, Mrs. Lanier says she wants to make her husband's office atmosphere as much like home as possible. His office has lots of mahogany paneling with accent touches of red.

She has made her area look like a homey sitting room with a red lacquer antique desk, white armoire and a chic white couch with red pillows and vases full of red roses. Her office also has three television sets and a large collection of family pictures in silver frames.

"We stay at City Hall sometimes until eight at night or later. If I wasn't there, I'd never get to see him," she explains. "When he and the staff want to watch the six o'clock news, they come in my office and we all watch. That's why I have all these TV sets. I want everything as comfortable as I can make it for him."

The forty-five-year-old Mrs. Lanier says that it never occurred to her that she wouldn't be by the side of the sixty-seven-year-old mayor through his busy day, *every day*.

"A lot of the things I do for him, a secretary would ordinarily do. But if it's personal, I want to be the one to do it for him."

The space she is using would not have been used otherwise. Previously it was a storage room. But there was so much talk about the office she was occupying that the mayor announced that he would pay for her area.

"It's $202 a month," says Mrs. Lanier. "Bob calculated it down to the last penny." Mayor Lanier says he continues to want his wife at his side. If this is a New South marriage, he's all for it.

Mrs. Lanier is known for her warm, outgoing personality and has a reputation as an exceptionally good hostess. She also once had a successful business of her own, selling trendy jewelry to Houston's rich and famous. But when she married Mr. Lanier, she took on duties at his land development company much like those she has at City Hall. So she was particularly hurt and puzzled when her new office caused such an uproar in Houston. After all, her interest goes far beyond City Hall.

She says she's an essential part of her husband's life

and should be by his side. It's the way she thinks a marriage should work.

"Bob has no interest in clothes whatsoever," she explains. "Every morning I pick out everything he is going to wear and lay it out for him. Before he became mayor, he picked out his own shoes and socks. But now he is so busy, I even do that."

This partnership continues to be discussed. Cab drivers and other blue-collar workers worry that Mrs. Lanier could never understand the poor and struggling. But working women send letters of admiration and support. Despite all the hoopla, her husband is just glad she is right there next to him.

Still others point out that it's particularly wise and shrewd of her to move with him into City Hall. This is one political wife who knows exactly where her husband is, and exactly what he's doing.

*A New Partnership: Bob and Elyse Lanier.* © Ed Lee

## Chapter Two

# Could Scarlett Have Been Codependent?

Southern women today spend a lot of time analyzing themselves. They still love being flirtatious. They still love dressing up. But when they read *Gone With the Wind,* they aren't as tolerant as their mothers were over Scarlett's fixation with Ashley Wilkes. Talk about a dysfunctional relationship. That wasn't love, that was an addiction. I personally think that Scarlett was terrific. But I can't help but wonder what she would be like today—out in the business world and with a good therapist.

—A Mobile woman on how women have changed in the New South

All Southern girls who were brought up by Southern-belle mothers were not automatically attracted to lace dresses and picking out silver patterns.

"I was taught to be strong," says Anne Herndon, who grew up in Tallahassee, Florida. "But my mother thought you could be just as strong being a majorette and twirling a baton as you could shooting baskets on the girls basketball team. She said it was the discipline that really counted.

"I had a good education, which I adored, but I also took drill team and baton lessons that I just hated. It's not that my mother didn't want me to learn. She just thought it was adorable to be in pageants and wear costumes. I'd rather be off somewhere reading a good book."

Anne says she was a tall, lean brunette in a drill team world of dimpled, blue-eyed blondes.

"When I got accepted to Harvard, my father was ecstatic. My mother was crushed. She thought there were very fine schools in the South where I wouldn't be tempted to become any more of a radical than I already was.

"As for me, I couldn't have been happier. Academically, I knew it would be challenging, but I didn't know of any group in Cambridge, Massachusetts, that would require me to twirl a baton before I was asked to join."

When she went to work in Philadelphia after graduating, Anne says she got into a therapy group.

"The first thing the therapist asked me was, 'Are you here because you're depressed?' I said, 'Not at all—I'm here because I'm Southern.'"

## The Fried Green Tomatoes

The Fried Green Tomatoes is a support group for restless Southern belles in Little Rock, Arkansas. They want to learn to be more up front and less devious with men.

"And that's not easy when you've been raised to be a Southern belle," says Alice Cockrell Allred, a direct descendant of Robert E. Lee. "It's not that we don't like being Southern. We love it. And we intend to keep all the charm and good manners. But we do need help in getting rid of some of that traditional Southern-belle subservience. We get kind of wild during these sessions, but we have a lot to overcome."

Alice says her mother (who is still beautiful at seventy-three) was famous for having been pinned to a boy in every fraternity at the University of Arkansas—all at the same time.

"Mother could handle it," Alice says. "But this is a different world today. Women have different roles. Juggling ten men at once is not considered the virtue it once was."

Not that her mother disapproves of new ways. She told Alice long ago that she could join any group she wanted, as long as she pledged Chi Omega in college.

Alice's mother even came to one of The Fried Green Tomato sessions.

"But she left early because she had to go home and watch Frank Sinatra on TV," Alice explains.

The Fried Green Tomatoes (after the Fannie Flagg novel and the movie of the same name) is a part of St. Margaret's Episcopal Church. They meet weekly and spend a lot of time examining their Southernness.

The fifteen members are in all different professions, including everything from doctors to a restaurant owner. Alice is a travel agent. One of the members was even voted one of the four outstanding women in Arkansas.

*The Fried Green Tomatoes of Little Rock, Arkansas.*

"We met in a movie complex. There were six theaters there and we never knew which one we'd get from week to week.

"We'd have to identify our weekly place by the movie playing. So the bulletin would say that the worship services will be held at *Terminator 2*, children's Sunday School will be at *Fantasia*. New church members got confused. To help them remember, the priest would send popcorn around to the houses with 'St. Margaret's Church' on the bag."

Alice says that this kind of atmosphere made it easy to start The Fried Green Tomatoes.

The group was the idea of one of the members who is a psychiatrist. Alice says she got interested because it

It's a pretty progressive group for the usually traditional Episcopal Church.

"When we first started The Fried Green Tomatoes, we didn't even have a church built yet," she explains.

isn't easy for a Southern woman of her age group and background to communicate without fluttering her eyelashes and chattering nonstop.

"I don't understand what we're exactly supposed to be learning," one of The Fried Green Tomatoes said at one session.

"It means," said Alice, "that when a man asks you the time, you tell him the time. You don't ramble on and on about how to make the watch."

"Oh my God, do I ramble like that?" asked the other Fried Green Tomato. "Is that why my boss's eyes glaze over when I try to explain things to him?"

The Fried Green Tomatoes do a lot of research to help their cause. One week they were discussing the book *Smart Cookies Don't Crumble.* The next they were learning how to keep a journal to interpret their dreams.

"And just to make sure things were balanced," she points out, "we invited Mrs. Arkansas in to talk to us."

Alice says despite all the liberating talk, the group is still Southern to their fingertips. Scarlett O'Hara would feel right at home in their midst, but Rhett Butler might just get a little bit defensive.

## The Scarlett O'Hara's

Donna Beard says she formed The Scarlett O'Hara Club to be the most upscale singles club in Atlanta. But she wants you to know there's nothing fiddle-dee-dee about them. They resent it if you even suggest it.

Donna says these Atlanta belles don't spend time worrying about tomorrow. They are strictly a *today* bunch of women. They call themselves The Scarletts because they respect Scarlett O'Hara for her beauty, brains and tenacity. They feel she would have fit right into their group.

But even Scarlett just couldn't breeze right in. This club has strict membership policies. Going out for The Scarletts is like being rushed for a sorority.

"This is a club for successful career women. Women

*The Scarlett O'Haras of Atlanta, Georgia.*

who need to meet men who are at their own intellectual level. Men who have good professions," Donna points out. "Only women who are established in executive positions or top professions are considered. Even the flight attendants who are members have second jobs as interior decorators."

Their guests also have to be the kind of men who have tuxedos to wear to formal parties. These men have to fit into the trendy, glitzy entertainments The Scarletts seem fondest of. But most of all, the men can't be married or even legally separated. They must be divorced or single. Nothing in between.

The Scarletts, in turn, invite their male guests to parties that echo the lifestyle the members forever hope to embody.

They do like to go to fancy places.

They do like extravagant lifestyles. But Donna is a bit touchy over a story about The Scarletts that had the headline, "I'll never go dutch again."

The Scarletts admit they like nice things and men who take them to nice places, but "we're not gold diggers," she emphasizes. "We just like to surround ourselves with successful people. And successful people go for the best."

Guests to The Scarletts' parties arrive via chauffeured Rolls-Royces and limousines. As guests enter whichever Southern mansion is on loan to the group for the evening, they walk through room after beautiful room filled with dozens of red roses, a dazzling array of cuisine and an elegant assortment of Atlanta singles.

"The Scarletts have a name in Atlanta," Donna says. "We don't have trouble finding the right places for our parties. It's all about that indefinable thing called *class*."

Donna came to Atlanta from Tulsa. She has always had her own flamboyant style. She's a strawberry blonde with a candy-apple-red mink coat who owns a Mercedes, a Rolls-Royce and a Jaguar.

She did lots of volunteer work when she first hit town and was considered a dynamo in the work she did for the arts. She's had two rich husbands, but the money she's got now she says she made herself.

At one time, she owned eleven stores that sold imported Chinese furniture. "I still own part of a warehouse in Hong Kong," she says, "but other than that I'm retired. I got burned out and I've got enough money to do other things."

She started The Scarletts four years ago when she decided women in her circle needed to meet more intellectual men and in places with a higher profile than bars. Members are voted in. She wanted to be certain the club was exclusive enough to attract "the right kind of people."

When the charter was written up, she made sure there were strict rules that would keep the club's members at a certain social and economic level.

For instance, when a Scarlett brings hors d'oeuvres to a party, her contribution has to arrive on a *silver* platter. That silver tray is a rule and shouldn't be a problem for a good Southern belle, even one who's a CEO.

As a prelude to a boat party The Scarletts were having, Donna wrote personal letters to all the members who were bringing friends to be considered as new members of The Scarletts.

"The qualities a new member must have are beauty, class, a good profession, enthusiasm for the club and an ability to pay dues. . . . It's your responsibility as a Scarlett to actively solicit new members. However, please do not embarrass The Scarletts or yourself by inviting someone who does not have these qualities."

Scarletts are between the ages of twenty-five and forty. Male guests are between thirty and fifty. The Scarletts are mostly blonde and love to sparkle. One guest remarked after his initial visit to a Scarlett party, "There could not have been a sequin left in all of Atlanta."

The Scarletts have had success in the romance department. At least a half-dozen members have found husbands or fiancés through club functions.

The reputation of The Scarletts is spreading at such a rate that a group of women in Pittsburgh want to start their own chapter.

Scarlett O'Hara in *Pittsburgh!*

"I just don't know," says Donna. "But after all these *are* new times."

## Southern Belles for Safer Sex

Delegates to the 1992 Republican National Convention did a real double take as they entered the convention area one morning.

Stretched across the median strip on the street outside the convention hall was a group of Southern belles dressed in traditional picture hats and hoop skirts. They looked like they were taking part in an Azalea Festival coronation.

Only, good heavens, these belles were not at any coronation. They were handing out color-coordinated *condoms*.

"Our group is called 'Southern Belles for Safer Sex,' " explained Toni Knight of Houston, peering from under a white ruffled hat.

"We're the Republicans' worst nightmare. We have

*Southern Belles for*
*Safer Sex.*

© *Dallas Morning News,*
Paula Nelson

good jobs, good manners, good wardrobes and we are pro-choice and pro-family planning."

You could almost smell the magnolias. They even carried flower baskets. But instead of roses and lilacs, the baskets were filled with pastel-colored condoms.

"You can tell we're belles," said a gracious woman in pink ruffles. "Our condoms are color-coordinated."

The belles were quite a traffic stopper. They handed out condoms to every delegate they could stop. One hoop-skirted woman said she handed a condom packet to a man she was sure was Michael Deaver.

"He took it and smiled," she said. "I think he thought it was mints."

"We want y'all to have a nice safe convention," the woman in pink ruffles said to a delegate. "Be safe now, you hear?"

"Here's a nice blue packet," one belle said to a man in a blue Buick. "It matches your car."

The leader of Southern Belles for Safer Sex is Tina Hester of the Pro-Choice Coalition of Kentucky. She says the belles made their first appearance at the Kentucky Derby, where they were immensely popular.

"Rhett Butler was no fool. He would have practiced safer sex," said a belle in a floral print dress just dripping in ribbons.

One Republican delegate was confused. She thought the costumed belles were a hospitality committee.

"Is this where you get the bus back to the hotel?" she asked.

"No," said a sweet-voiced belle, "this is where you get your condoms."

The delegate was appalled.

The Southern Belles for Safer Sex continue to make appearances at major events all over the South.

They continue to be belle-like, even when some people tell them they are a disgrace to Southern womanhood.

"I don't care if y'all do have on lace and hoop skirts," one man told them, "you are *not* ladies. Why, I never thought I'd see the day."

The safer-sex belles say they are too committed to back down. They will keep starching their hoop skirts and delivering their message.

And fiddle-dee-dee. Scarlett had her detractors too.

## Chapter Three

# Tomorrow Is Another Day! But Who Ever Thought Tomorrow Would Look Like This?

*A* lot of things have happened in my life that might have *surprised* my mother if she had lived to see them. But I think only one thing would have *shocked* her—that my husband walked out after twenty-eight years of marriage. In my mother's day, Southern gentlemen didn't do things like that. Eighteen years ago, I was the first to be divorced in my family. Now it's an epidemic.

—A North Carolina woman on divorce in the New South

## This Didn't Happen to Doris Day

Southern belles were brought up to believe in "happily ever after." If charm alone didn't work, they would always be able to get what they wanted by using their husband's name. And, of course, there would be a husband. This, after all, was the South.

"For years I did get what I needed by using my husband's name," says one belle. "Then one day he didn't want to be married anymore. Soon there was a second Mrs. Smith. Then there was a third Mrs. Smith. There were too many Mrs. Smiths. I took back my maiden name and went to work."

But it isn't just being single again that made life different. It was discovering that everything you'd been brought up to believe in has changed.

"I was the fourth-generation woman in my family to make her debut," says one belle. "We're about as

34

Southern as you can be. I just assumed it would go on with my daughter and granddaughters. Well, my life didn't exactly turn out like they promised in cotillion. My daughter has just left a drug rehabilitation clinic. She says that was bad but not as bad as it would be to have a year-long debutante season. She just doesn't feel the same about all the old traditions. She says I could have handled her father a lot better if I wasn't so blinded by what my mother and grandmother wanted me to believe was true."

Her ex-husband is married again to a woman he met at a business convention. She is not Southern.

"My husband always told me I had 'Southern damage.' He thinks Southern women are impossible to live with because they will never find a man who treats them like their daddy did. I say Southern women have problems because they've had to live with Southern men."

But if there is one thing the Old South woman learned from her grandmother it was how to be tough. True, steel magnolias get bruised, but basically they're still steel magnolias. It's just that there is a lot to cope with in the 1990s—even if you were the prettiest girl who ever bowed at the Camellia Debutante Ball.

In the past, Southern belles taught their daughters to marry well. These days, they're more pragmatic. They're telling them to divorce well.

Alice Twiggs Vantrease lives in one of the most historic homes in Beaufort, South Carolina. There is an original cannon from the Civil War in her den—and it still faces North.

"I was raised as a typical Southern belle, but a divorce made me see I was going to have to be tough and take charge of my own life."

She now has a successful business and makes frequent speeches to women's groups about facing reality in the New South. She calls it "Getting Out of the Velvet Ghetto."

She bases her New South philosophy on what she learned from her Old South grandmother who told her, "Get up every day and consider the stage you're on. Only you can decide whether it will be a tragedy, a comedy or a drama."

## For Better or Worse, For Rich or Richer

Houston philanthropist Carolyn Farb says she was very helpful to her multimillionaire husband, Harold, during the years they were married.

She renovated a rather ordinary mansion and turned it into a showplace to dazzle his friends. She encouraged him to sing on his own record albums, which she produced and gave as favors at their parties. She promoted million-dollar charity balls where Harold rubbed shoulders with movie stars and high society.

"And even though we had a house full of servants," she said at the time of the divorce, "I always looked after him myself. I saw to it that he was very pampered. I ban-ished chicken from the house because he hates chicken. I personally went to the bakery and bought his favorite pineapple pies. And when he went on trips, I always packed his bags myself.

"Before I met Harold, he was just known as a man who built apartments. After we were together, I gave his life a kind of magic. It was like living a fantasy. That should be worth something."

It was.

In 1983, Carolyn and Harold Farb had one of the most high-profile divorces ever in Houston, Texas. The then forty-three-year-old Carolyn was reported to receive more than $20 million in a property settlement that included the couple's River Oaks mansion, two Rolls-Royces, a Jaguar and a reported $8 million in cash. The couple had been married only *six* years.

At the time, Harold was reported to be worth $167 million. The divorce included a court case that knocked down a prenuptial agreement signed by Carolyn that would have limited her settlement to scarcely more than $1 million. Her attorney, Bob Piro, stated that it was not the biggest property settlement ever made in Texas, "but considering the length of the marriage it was extraordinary."

Carolyn says, "It wasn't the money. It was the spirit of the thing. He thought every minute I would buckle under and give in. I went to court quivering and shaking but I was determined. We brought an economist into court with charts showing how much Harold prospered during our marriage. I had a lot to do with that prosperity. I inspired him.

"I'm not a women's libber, but I think when I won that case, I did something that has given women all over the country new hope. I did this for women everywhere."

After their marriage in 1977, Carolyn began entertaining lavishly, and pictures of the couple appeared regularly in newspapers and magazines. But she said the balls and parties she organized for charity were her passion.

In a sworn deposition, Harold said his wife lived in a "dreamworld." Living with her was like living with a movie star. She never came down to earth.

"There was no satisfying Carolyn. I'd buy her a small

*Carolyn Farb with Jim Nabors at one of her charity functions.*

ring or a small necklace and she'd say it was beautiful," he said in the deposition. "Then she would take the small jewels and trade them in for bigger ones." He also didn't like going out every night.

"I'm a down-to-earth person and I've had enough," he said. "The Museum of Fine Arts Ball almost drove me crazy. We had the equivalent of a switchboard in our home and all the phone calls and strange people coming in and out.

"When I married her, she wanted to be Mrs. Harold Farb," Harold testified. "Now she wants to be Carolyn Farb. It's just too much. What's wrong with a husband wanting a wife to be a wife?"

Carolyn did not give up on her charity endeavors. She continues to raise millions of dollars every year in Houston. She says she puts the same energy and creativity into her fund-raising as she put into her marriage.

"I started networking when I was a teenager," she says. "I always have a pen and pencil ready and ideas are constantly evolving. I continue until the work is completed. The days extend beyond the normal eight-hour routine. I have organized piles of clutter extending from the bedroom to any desk space available."

In the line of duty, she has worked with everyone from Marvin Hamlisch to Henry Kissinger. Now she wants to share all this with others. She has written a book called *How to Raise Millions, Helping Others, Having a Ball.*

"In this book I have shared my rewarding experiences as a volunteer fundraiser. I hope to educate the public about how they too can become a part of this vital activity in our country. I hope this will motivate others to have the courage and adventurousness it requires."

## Let Me Direct You
## To The Right Place

Some women have found their Southern-belle training to be useless after thirty years of marriage. Others say, don't be ridiculous. It's just as valuable now as it's ever been. They just have to change their focus.

"I wasn't going to give up all those years of lists and charity-ball contacts," says one woman. "I found that all those new people moving in had lots of ambition but not much social know-how. At least for the way things are done around here."

She takes newcomers on as clients.

"I teach the wives how to dress for sultry summer lun-cheons. I tell the husbands which country clubs to join and help them get invited. I also help get their daughters in the right sororities. It takes a lot of contacts and a lot of just knowing the ropes."

Her services don't come cheap. A real social overhaul can cost $10,000.

"Why should I give away what took me forty-five years to learn for just a few hundred dollars? But they are willing to pay. I am an important link from the old to the new."

She says even her ex-husband has sought out her ser-vices. She had the social connections. He had the money. They have been divorced for twenty years. His new wife doesn't have the right connections.

"He's got daughters who need to get the right recom-mendations for sororities and debuts," she explains. "He's discreetly asked me to help. My best friend says it's a perfect time to get him back for all the misery he caused me."

But she was raised as a Southern belle and Southern belles have better ways of getting even. It still works very well in the New South.

"I'm going to help those girls all I can. But I'm going to make sure they let their mother know just who is doing it. She can't turn down the help. The daughters are too important to her. But just knowing I was involved will be enough to make her furious with her husband. He'll be more miserable this way than he ever would have been if I had just said no."

*The Magnolia Charity Ball Committee requests
the pleasure of your company
for
a seated dinner and dance
Saturday the eighth of February
at half after seven o'clock in the evening*

*Willow Falls Country Club*

*R.S.V.P.
card enclosed*

*White or
Black Tie*

## We Never Talked About Things Like This

In the old days, Southern women often had attacks of "nerves." There were no Betty Ford clinics then, just hospitals and spas that helped you get over crying jags or drying out from alcohol. There was no stigma involved because everyone at these genteel places dressed for dinner. Each woman could feel she was with "her own kind."

"Lots of us had to go off for our nerves," says one woman. "If it wasn't a real serious condition, these little trips even helped. It was like group therapy, only we didn't realize it was therapy. We'd just sit around and talk about our problems. Then we'd take afternoons off and go shopping."

But some people had attacks of more than just nerves. That was something that no one liked to look at too closely.

Betty Shirley certainly shouldn't have had any problems. Her life in Tuscaloosa, Alabama, appeared to be perfect. She had a lovely time in college, joined the right sorority, married a man who became president of the bank and was a pillar of *old Tuscaloosa* society.

Mental illness was never discussed, not even when she started having problems when she was a senior in college. Just taking a final exam brought on undue stress. Back in 1948, she was assumed to be one of those women with "nerves."

In 1952, after she had her first child, Mrs. Shirley was so depressed she was given shock therapy. Things got worse in 1968. A doctor she respected suggested something radical. She should go for treatment at Bryce Hospital, the state mental hospital in Tuscaloosa.

"The doctor I needed was there," she says. "But a state hospital was not the place a president of the bank sent his wife. It was very courageous of George."

The treatments helped and Mrs. Shirley could have gone on with her sheltered life without anyone knowing too much about what she was going through. A strong Southern woman, she chose not to. She became very involved with mental health in her community.

"It was nothing to be ashamed of," she said. "I realized a lot of things just weren't the way I was brought up to believe."

When a grandson was diagnosed with Down's syndrome, she became involved in that too. Because of her work, President Bush named her one of his Thousand Points of Light.

Mrs. Shirley also never stopped being a Southern belle and has even managed to combine being a belle with her activism.

As a member of the Tuscaloosa Mental Health Board, there's always a need to raise money. A few years ago, the committee decided to do Tuscaloosa's first decorator showcase house. Local decorators would turn a historic old home into a showplace that people would pay to come and view.

First, they had to find the house.

Betty said she knew just the place. The superintendent's home on the grounds of Bryce Hospital.

*"The mental hospital?"* some of the other members said in shock. "You can't do a showcase at the mental hospital."

"Why not?" said Betty. "The place is empty at the moment and it's a lovely home on lovely grounds."

Betty had clout. The house turned out to be exquisite. The showcase was a huge success.

"I just sat on a rocker on the front porch and watched people coming," she says. "I had to laugh. For most it was the first time they'd ever been to a place like this."

The house was so beautifully done that the group decided to keep it and rent it out for parties. There wasn't anything like it anywhere else in Tuscaloosa.

"It's so Southern," she explains. "It's a lovely two-story building with balconies and columns. A real dream house. Some brides balked at first about having their wedding parties there, but not for long."

One young socialite gave a party there but says she didn't know how to explain to her mother in Virginia that she was giving a party at a mental institution.

"So I just wrote her that the party was going to be in a lovely floral setting that lots of Southerners could identify with. My mother was very happy. She loves tradition."

Chapter Four

# The New Players

*The* names of the banks in Dallas are changing so fast, I don't even know where to send invitations to ask for corporate sponsors for our charity gala. I knew Republic Bank had become NCNB Bank. But I'd hardly put NCNB on the list when I was told it was now being called Nation's Bank. I fretted about this until my cousin told me I was just going to have to stop worrying and find some new sponsors. Forget the banks, the land developers and the oilmen who were our old sponsors. They can't come to the parties anymore; they're all in bankruptcy court. The people who are buying those charity tickets today are the plastic surgeons and the plumbing contractors.

—The Dallas charity ball chair lamenting
the changing economic and social scene in Texas

## When Bubba Starts Wearing Armani, We Call Him Buddy

We all know Bubba from the Old South. He raises a lot of hell, drinks a lot of beer and has a gun rack on the back of his pickup truck. Bubba is a piece of work and has always been good copy up north. He was considered a factor in the 1992 presidential campaign and was often discussed on the network news. Reporters loved to focus on "the Bubba vote," particularly in the primaries.

That was fun, but really a waste of time—Bubba doesn't vote in the primaries. Bubba thinks a primary is the first coat of paint you put on when you're painting the pickup. Bubba rarely votes at all.

This is the 1990s. What we're dealing with now is "the Buddy vote." Buddy is a Bubba with a master's degree and a condo he can't sell. Buddy is very mad about all that negative cash flow, so these days he talks as much about political change as he does about who is going to win the Southeastern Conference football title.

Yes, just like Bubba, Buddy loves football. But Buddy isn't cracking an iced one with his fellow couch potatoes while he waits for the kickoff. He watches games from an air-conditioned corporate skybox and washes down his chicken-fried steak (fried only in pure vegetable oil) with imported designer water. Buddy's first wife won the talent preliminary in the Miss Mississippi Pageant by twirling a double-fire baton. His second wife is chairing the Symphony League Ball.

# How Bubbette Got to Be Barbara

When the media was making so much fuss about Bubba, they made a big mistake. They forgot all about one major factor—Bubbette.

It's true, Bubbette spent a lot of time in the background. For years, she devoted herself to taking care of Bubba, cooking his pot roasts and making dip for the bowling league auxiliary. She also sold cosmetics on the side. But when nobody was looking, Bubbette took all that money she made selling cosmetics and went to law school at night.

Now Bubbette has become Barbara and she's running the Democratic and Republican precincts. She is very power-ful. Even Bubba is beginning to understand that. Not that Barbara is still with Bubba. They divorced six years ago. She's now living with her nutritionist. He's thirty-five. She's forty-two.

Some of Barbara's more traditional friends think that she's given up the essence of being a Southern woman because of some of her recent activities. Ridiculous. Barbara may be too busy to cook anymore (she brings home a lot of take-out from the Jitney Jungle), but she has never forgotten what she learned back in her sixth-grade Etiquette for the Ages classes: She always serves her take-out food with cloth napkins.

# The Miss Maybelle Factor

It's easy for young people to get all caught up in the New South, but for traditional Southern ladies like Miss Maybelle, it's quite a different matter.

Miss Maybelle wouldn't dream of serving those miniature quiches you buy at Sam's Warehouse; she still bakes her Cheese Straws fresh for company. And she doesn't approve of anyone named Madonna outside of the church.

Miss Maybelle is eighty-two and a pillar of the local garden club. She's not usually a political person, but she does admit she watched every bit of the Clarence Thomas hearings on TV.

She thought the language was awful, particularly when they discussed the part involving Anita Hill. Miss Maybelle couldn't believe such carryings-on would be discussed on TV. As far as she could see, it was just plain trashy.

She was particularly appalled when a very vocal feminist came on one show and loudly proclaimed, "It's time we women started to kick some ass." *Ass* is not a word Miss Maybelle is used to hearing bandied about on TV.

Her granddaughters tried to explain that no one was being intentionally vulgar. It was just that women were being treated shabbily and people needed to see that.

Miss Maybelle would not be moved. She thinks ladies should be, first and foremost, ladies, and that the issue of women's rights should be approached with ladylike manners and respect. Miss Maybelle thinks it's time to kick a little *fanny*.

# Glad to Meet Y'all, I'm Kenneth

There are a lot of Kenneths in the New South. They did not come by choice. Kenneth is an executive who was transferred from Connecticut. During his first year, Kenneth constantly wrote letters to old friends complaining that his Southern friends put mayonnaise on their corned beef sandwiches. That is, when they could *find* corned beef sandwiches.

Kenneth didn't move into a traditional Southern neighborhood, but bought a large two-story brick home in a new subdivision, with five bathrooms, each one bigger than his front yard, and a security guard.

Gradually, Kenneth's letters to Connecticut stopped sounding so distressed. Two years later, when he went back to New Haven for a family reunion, he was lamenting that there was no cornbread stuffing in his Aunt Priscilla's turkey. He's stopped saying "you guys" and now refers to groups as "y'all."

Kenneth was told he'd have a hard time breaking into old-line Southern society, but that just wasn't the case. Shortly after he arrived, three prominent, native-born city fathers got indicted for savings-and-loan fraud. Kenneth could pick any civic and philanthropic organization he wanted to join (as long as his company was willing to be a corporate sponsor).

Kenneth's company is now a major supporter of the Magnolia Charity Ball (which raises money to fight diseases in children). That's where he met his new wife, Mary Ashley, who was the gala's dessert chairwoman. Mary Ashley calls him Kenny. He calls her at least five times a day.

## That Shannon Is a Whirlwind

The Shannons in the New South are second wives from places like California. Shannon met her Southern husband when they were both attending a business seminar at Duke University.

Shannon is the first to admit it was difficult moving into a small Southern town where everyone was kin to her husband's first wife. But she didn't let it get her down.

She is a venture capitalist, so she has plenty to do, even though she wasn't asked to join the Junior Auxiliary. Instead she did something bold: She became a Rotarian.

Shannon may not be Old South, but she's still become a force to be reckoned with. Her pearls are fake, but her money is real. In the New South that counts for a lot. She has also learned some of the old rules. Her home is always available for invitation-addressing parties for museum fund-raisers. She is in her sixth year as head of the welcoming committee for the annual Christmas Arts Festival and Nutcracker Gala.

And she plans always to be on those committees, at least until her child gets through Ole Miss. She says she'll be damned if being from San Jose is going to get in the way of her daughter getting a bid to a good sorority.

## You're Going to Hear a Lot About Nathaniel

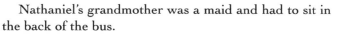

Nathaniel's grandmother was a maid and had to sit in the back of the bus.

His mother went to a teachers college and saw to it that he got a scholarship to Yale.

Nathaniel is now a lawyer in the same firm as the grandson of the man for whom his grandmother worked for twenty-five years.

Nathaniel went through a period of trying to be more New England than the New Englanders. But now he's come home and he's comfortable with his roots. Forget all that foie gras; Nathaniel's back to serving his grand-mother's recipes—only now he serves those black-eyed peas and hominy on Wedgwood china.

His cousin Melba takes this even further. She serves their grandmother's collard greens, fried chicken and corn bread at her trendy East Side restaurant in New York City. She says her grandmother served this food because it was good and cheap, though it's *not* cheap in Melba's restaurant.

Suddenly, turnip greens are considered very chic. Melba says her grandmother has got to be in heaven, laughing her head off.

## Gentlemen, Start Your Engines . . . and Your Barbeque Grills!

In the South, football stadium skyboxes may be considered the ultimate in extravagance, but wait until you see what Burton Smith has done at the Charlotte Motor Speedway.

Smith is about as New South as you can get in Charlotte. He doesn't do his business entertaining on the traditional golf courses and in the traditional country clubs. Smith owns the Motor Speedway. He loves the track and he adores spending a lot of his time there. So one day he figured he should do it in style.

"I knew football stadiums were doing very well with their skyboxes for people to watch games in. These had all the touches of home, but they weren't home. So I thought, 'Why not?' "

Smith then started building condominiums, right on the racetrack.

That's right, his front yard is the first turn. Where some people would plant petunias, Smith's high-rise condo, First Turn Tower, looks down on grandstands.

A lot of *Old* Charlotte thought he was out of his mind. Not only did he want to build these condos, he was going to charge $90,000 for this ridiculousness.

Poor man. Didn't he understand? You build your second home at the beach. On a golf course. Maybe the mountains. *Not* at a racetrack.

But Smith had the last laugh. The condos sold like crazy. The original $90,000 units are now reselling for $300,000 and a whole new condo tower has just gone up with prices that reach almost a half-million dollars for penthouses.

"People didn't believe it at first," Burton says. "But I love racing and I know a lot of other people do. There's no thrill like waking up on a race morning and

*The new Tara in Atlanta—Tara Place at the Atlanta Speedway.*

seeing it all from your living-room window."

Obviously, many race enthusiasts think so too. The condos have been snapped up by businessmen, doctors, race-car drivers and just plain sports fans who want to savor every aspect of race-car driving. Some live there full-time. Some consider it a second home or a vacation home. And why not? The speedway is so much closer than the ocean.

Smith, who is also a Ford dealer in Charlotte, says living at the track makes partying at a mere skybox seem like going to a children's birthday party.

At his condos, you can eat, drink and sleep race-car driving. You can even take a bath or bake cookies without losing your front-row seat. And, oh, the thrill of barbecuing out on your deck as the crowd is going crazy at the height of a roaring NASCAR race.

And who needs curtains when your entire living room is a glass wall onto the track?

Loy and Elizabeth Allen's penthouse unit has two bedrooms, two baths, chandeliers and mirrored ceilings, not to mention a marble Jacuzzi tub. It's a real extravagance, but Loy says it's worth it. It's a great place to do business.

Just what does he do to afford such racetrack luxury?

"Small business, big cash flow," explains a track observer. "Those are the kinds of people who have the money today."

Loy Allen is the owner of a Raleigh, North Carolina, company called Precision Walls. His customers *adore* being invited to the track. And because living at the speedway is a fantasy, the decor does a lot to perpetuate this fantasy. The sleek white, chrome and mirrored condo has a spiral staircase; purple, green and lavender accents; and a television set that rises right out of a table. Plush banquette sofas for viewing the races are stretched across the entire living room.

And when you get tired of looking at the racetrack, you can always stare up at the ceiling, which is done up with stars to simulate the galaxy.

"At night, the ceiling seems to just blend into the sky outside," Allen explains. "People really like it."

The two bedrooms in the racetrack unit have lots of built-in touches. One bathroom has a faucet that spouts like a waterfall.

"My wife saw that faucet in the movie *Sleeping With the*

*Enemy,"* says Loy. "We tracked it down so we could put it in here." He looks at the gold faucet and starts to laugh. "When I was a kid on the farm, we used to get that same effect when we used a pump to get water. But that's what she wanted, so we got it."

These glitzy condos have certainly attracted a lot of attention. But they are by no means the only upscale offerings to be found at the speedway.

"We are now doing black-tie parties right on the track," says marketing director Jane Allen. "We've even had the symphony playing at these events. We really put on the Ritz."

Jane was raised a traditional Southern belle just ten miles down the road and she says the speedway has changed enormously since then.

*Interior of the Loy Allen Condo at the Charlotte Motor Speedway.*

"My mother always lectured me, 'Don't ever get involved with those people at the track.' If she were alive today, I can't imagine what she would think. I met and fell in love with a race-car driver from Illinois. We had to sneak around to date.

"Who would have ever thought it. Now I'm a grandmother in sports marketing. Mother would have been absolutely horrified. Or then again, maybe she wouldn't. I am in a $20 million building. I only entertain CEOs and other top executives, and last year I sold $2.6 million in sponsorships."

The speedway's owner is absolutely delighted to see his Charlotte venture doing so well. But Smith explains that he's certainly not going to rest on his laurels.

He thinks his racetrack condos are a phenomenon that are going to get more and more popular in the New South. Just wait until you see what he has in store for the speedway he owns in Atlanta.

These condos will have Georgian columns. Not easy to do on a speedway high-rise, but his marketing people say it will look very "Georgian modern." Scheduled to open in 1994, the prices will hover at around a half-million dollars. The front yard will be the speedway. But there will also be swimming pools, tennis courts and a fitness club.

And, oh yes, there will be one other Georgian touch. Smith is calling it Tara Place.

# Why the Russians Were Shocked in Louisville!

Sixty-five-year-old Lucie Becker Blodgett has had three husbands, seven children and a twenty-year stint as a society writer for the *New Voice* newspaper in Louisville, Kentucky.

Lucie has seen it all in Old South society and she's watched the arrival of New South society. The new ways are certainly different.

In the old days, when stories of the most prominent Louisville families were written, it was for their parties, lifestyles and comings and goings.

If the prestigious *Louisville Courier Journal* wrote about anything scandalous on its society pages, it was only vaguely gossipy. "Maybe a scandal would be if someone broke into one of the fine old homes," she recalls. "Then the story would be written with style and good taste."

Today books and magazines have chronicled stories of the most intimate nature about even the Bingham family,

one of Louisville's most prominent families and the former owners of the *Courier Journal.* Tales of sex, greed and family deceptions abound; *no* detail has been spared.

Even the Binghams' many employees didn't talk openly about such goings-on years ago. Now they can turn on the TV and hear the most torrid stories about their former bosses freely discussed—and during the dinner hour, no less.

"That breaks my heart," Lucie says. "Mr. Bingham was my first boss at the *Louisville Courier* and he was a wonderful man. I have only the highest respect for that family."

She admits things have changed. Even some perceptions of traditional, well-mannered Louisville have changed.

"Not long ago I quoted a group of visiting Russians as saying that there was language being used in live theater productions in Louisville that would be considered too vulgar to put on the stage in Russia."

That raised some eyebrows. Just five years ago, Communism was still considered a threat in Louisville. Not many had ever met a Russian, much less discussed manners with them, but you can be sure that if the subject had come up, Louisville would have laughed at the idea of tak-

*Lucie Blodgett—society columnist who has covered both the Old and the New South.* © John Nation

ing etiquette pointers from Leningrad.

Lucie made sure their remarks were in her column.

"I mean, who would have ever thought Russia would tell Louisville how to be ladylike?" she says.

She explains that these were Russian drama critics who had come to see premieres of new plays at the Actor's Theater of Louisville, a prestigious regional theater that has a worldwide reputation for showcasing new playwrights. The Pulitzer Prize–winning plays *The Gin Game* and *Crimes of the Heart* were first produced there before they went to Broadway.

"The director," says Lucie, "is *very* avant-garde. He presents a world that's not my world, but it's out there and it should be portrayed. They do, however, use an awful lot of the *F* word."

The changes in the theater world is one thing; that's to be expected. But she never thought she'd see so much change at such an Old South institution as Churchill Downs, the home of the Kentucky Derby.

"In the old days," she explains, "it was the fine old families of Louisville who had all the best seats and boxes in the third-floor clubhouse. These people kept Churchill Downs going and they were very influential. They were responsible for the Derby.

"But now, when the owner of a box dies, that box does

not automatically get passed down to his family. Many are taken away and sold to big-business people. My husband's grandfather had three Derby winners, but my children could not inherit his box. Big-business and corporate sponsorship is everything now. With this new money, the Downs has expanded and they've added a lot of new facilities overlooking the track in places like Millionaires Row and the Turf Club. It's very nice, but it's just not the same. The people at Churchill Downs are going to kill me for saying this, but that's just the way it is. I look at those boxes now and they are occupied by people I have never heard of. They could as easily be from Las Vegas as Louisville."

Lucie emphasizes that she is not against progress per se, she just loves tradition. She says she was probably New South before anyone had ever heard of New South. When it came to living her life, she didn't think the only way to get ahead was to have a man take care of her.

"In 1961, I took my divorce money and bought a historic 1851 house out in the country with nine acres. It wasn't just a pretty Southern place to live. It was an investment. I paid $47,000 for it. Today it's appraised at $1.5 million.

"Those beautiful, elaborate springtime hats that women wear are a Derby tradition," she says. "It just wouldn't be the Derby without them."

New York designer Frank Olive flies into Louisville every year and does a trunk fashion show and benefit for the Kentucky Derby Museum.

"Everyone comes and selects their hats," Lucie explains. "It's always a big occasion."

She says Churchill Downs quietly makes sure even the new people are aware of the hat tradition.

"They had me call a lady horse owner in New York and explain that she was going to need a hat when she came for the race. I even told her where to buy it."

Lucie recalls that not long ago she bought a new Frank Olive hat for herself. It was a lovely pink creation.

"Before I could wear it, I found out I was going to require surgery. I wasn't sure how my medical problems were going to work out, but I have to tell you, that hat I never got to wear was really on my mind.

"I went to my minister and said, 'Don't think I'm crazy, but I have a great affection for that hat. I'm telling you right now, if I don't survive, I want that hat on me in the coffin. It's that important to me.' "

## Did We Meet in Athens, Greece . . . or Was It Athens, Texas?

When Lennox Samuels was named head of the "High Profile" section of the *Dallas Morning News*, local socialites were curious. The section is very prestigious and features profiles on who and what is currently prominent and successful in Texas. The editor guides social coverage and is the boss of the society writers. In other words, he wields a lot of power.

Quite a few people wanted to make sure they created a good impression on this new Mr. Samuels.

"Then I got this phone call early one morning," says a local socialite. "My friend was amazed. She said she finally found out who this Lennox Samuels was. She said I was never going to believe it. *He's black.*"

"*Black!*"

"*Black!*" she said. "I can't believe it. What are they doing to our section? Are they going to change it, try and make it politically correct? I wonder how he's going to look at the Crystal Charity Ball? What if he's radical? What's going to happen to coverage of our parties?"

Samuels was aware of all the talk. It amused him. He wryly notes that the initials of the "High Profile" section are the same as those of a very exclusive area in Dallas called Highland Park.

"A lot of them considered the section a Highland Park section," he says. "They were sure I was going to do an ethnic make-over."

The new society editor may have been new to the section, but he wasn't new to the *Dallas News*. He had been a projects editor on the city desk after coming to Texas from a paper in Wisconsin. Along with "High Profile," he would also be the editor of the paper's fashion section.

*Lennox Samuels, "High Profile" editor, at a social event with New Age musician Yanni (left).*

He is a frequent world traveler, and has now been named assistant managing editor for national and international coverage.

Before the social crowd met Samuels, some admitted they held their breaths.

"It was really hilarious," says the woman who made the first frantic phone call to her friend. "We were so worried he wasn't going to be our kind. We were prepared for *anything*.

"And he did shock us. What we didn't expect was a man who was so incredibly self-possessed that he could make *us* squirm. He was wearing Armani, driving a Porsche and had a beautiful British accent. We were charmed. People started knocking themselves out to invite him to parties. And this is where he surprised us again. He rarely accepted. He's perfectly charming. He just says no a lot."

Samuels, a former British citizen, was born in British Honduras (now Belize) and is the product of British boarding schools. He admittedly can be arrogant and explains, "I certainly wasn't worried about not being invited anywhere. And if I wasn't, so what? Whether I go to parties or not has nothing to do with how I run my section. I didn't have to break into those circles. I was famous for my own parties."

His nonchalant attitude only made him more in demand.

But Samuels says he prefers small, intimate gatherings to big social affairs. He'd rather deal with the glitzy community from his office.

"My goal," he explains, "was to turn 'High Profile' into the Dallas version of *Vanity Fair*." He started ordering tougher profiles featuring a more diverse collection of people. He also started going to Europe to cover the spring fashion collections.

One woman explains that one morning she personally delivered an invitation to a large charity ball to Samuels's office.

A receptionist told her Samuels was out of town.

"Well, he should leave wherever he is early, because I'm sure he will want to be in Dallas on Saturday night," the woman explained. "This is going to be a very big event."

"That would be a little difficult," she was told. "He's in Milan."

Chapter Five

# The Girls Are Becoming Women

My mother is seventy-eight and has finally stopped dyeing her hair. I asked her why she did this at this stage of the game. She says it's because her granddaughter is thirty-four and she's got gray hair. Mother doesn't fully approve of the young women letting their looks go like that. But she thinks it's unseemly to be blonder than your granddaughter.

—A Baton Rouge man on his mother's adjustment to the New South

A group of Southern women visiting New York were lunching at a popular restaurant filled with trendy Manhattan career women. After a while, a Nashville woman looked around and noted something was wrong, out of sync—she just couldn't grasp what it was.

Jerri Anne Lane stared a few minutes with a puzzled look on her face.

"I can tell you what it is," she finally said after a while. "Look at these women in here. They are all attractive and well dressed. Most of them look like they are in their thirties or early forties and more than half of them have gray hair. No Southern woman lets her hair go gray. There is more gray hair in this room than in all of Macon and Atlanta combined."

Everyone agreed that was true. One of the Southerners explained that back home one woman has even made her daughters promise that if their mother's roots need touching up when she dies, the daughters won't allow the coffin to be open.

"That's a true story," the woman said. "The woman is the mother of a friend of mine. Her mother says the last impression is the one everyone remembers you by. She was born a blonde and she is going to die with everyone remembering her as a blonde."

But in this room, the women didn't seem to mind being gray. They had long hair, short hair, mod hair, frizzled hair.

But there was definitely a lot of gray hair. The Southern women looked around the room and agreed: There really is a cultural gap between the North and the South.

Brenda Myron, forty-two, was seated at the next table. She's a stockbroker and has lived in New York City all her life. She has been partially gray since she was thirty-six. She wears her curly hair down to her shoulders. Brenda was amused at the conversation of the Southern women, which she admitted she couldn't help but overhear.

"I was just as overwhelmed when I went to a wedding in Atlanta two years ago," Brenda said. "Everyone there had blonde hair, including some of my relatives. My aunt and mother say absolutely no one in our family has ever been born blonde. We certainly knew all that blonde hair couldn't be real."

The Southerners just laughed. It never occurred to them to wonder if blonde hair is real blonde. They just assume it isn't. This started a long conversation on the pressures to dye your hair.

"It's a pain," said Anne Dawson, a homemaker from Dallas who doesn't like to give her age. "But I've been blonde since college." She looked at Brenda, the New Yorker, who was stylish and attractive. "See, on you I think it looks great," she said. "But a lot of people here are gray and you can feel good about it. In Dallas, it is a lot more deadly."

The Southern women admitted that they do know a few Southern women who go gray and look great.

"But in my group," explained Anne, "we all have husbands who like blonde hair. We talk about whether we should or should not color. Then we give out the names of the best hairdressers."

Brenda found that amusing.

"Don't men in the South have gray hair?" she asked.

Yes, but their mothers are blonde.

## I'm Here if You Need Me

But, of course, everyone isn't a blonde in the South, real or otherwise. Some Southern women go gray without a whimper. Others find they need a little help.

That's where Carla Kay comes in.

Carla is a Houston image consultant who knows all about this obsession Southern women have with being blonde. But she says this is the New South and it's time to admit that blondes don't always have more fun, or brunettes either for that matter. They just need a little liberating.

Carla has become sort of a guru to help Southern women go gray.

So if you've been trying desperately to let those gray roots grow out, but have anxiety attacks when watching old Farrah Fawcett reruns, Carla wants you to know there's someone out there who understands.

You can pick up the phone and call her Crisis Line for women who want to keep their natural hair color. She'll give you strength and support.

She says this obsession with being forever blonde or brunette is an addiction. And you can't miss the warning signs of women addicted to dye. They won't even go on a long vacation for fear their roots will begin to show somewhere between the Eiffel Tower and Buckingham Palace. And they repeatedly ruin the bathroom towels with dye while trying to cover their gray.

"I understand the feelings," says Carla. "I've been there myself." The attractive fifty-three-year-old now has dark hair heavily frosted with natural gray.

"I dyed my hair brown for years," she says. "I thought it made me look younger. But I'd look at other women and could always tell when their hair was dyed. It just didn't look natural. It was usually too harsh. I finally realized it was really making them look older.

"Since helping people look good is my business, I started to pay attention."

That's when she knew she needed to let her own hair turn gray.

"But it wasn't easy. This is Houston. Everywhere you look, there are blondes. I just couldn't let go."

That was thirteen years ago. She knew she had to take drastic measures.

At first, she formed a monthly support group for women who wanted to keep their natural hair color.

"We all just needed to talk about how we felt."

Some had what they considered mousy brown hair and had been keeping themselves blonde. Others, like Kay, were reluctant to go gray.

"It helps to tell horror stories about dyeing your hair," she says. "That way, instead of crying, we all have a good laugh."

One blonde told how she'd race to the beauty shop the day before going to a big football game, afraid that everyone seated above her would be looking down on her dark roots.

Other women talked of never wanting to walk in the wind—the wind might part the hair and show the gray.

"Then there were tales of ruined tile in the bathroom because of spilled dye on the floor," she says.

Carla would then launch into her testimonial. How she finally learned she could exist away from her hairdresser.

Carla is still preaching, but she admits she needs more role models. Trying to get the South to go gray is a full-time job.

She seeks help wherever she can find it. The image consultant says she spent a lot of time during the Reagans' White House years wishing that Nancy Reagan was urging people to say no to Clairol—while she was also urging them to say no to drugs.

## Hallelujah! She's Got a Crown . . . and She's Got Cellulite!

There was a firm rule in the Old South: Beauty queens were forever firm. They *never* got past the age of twenty-five (and that was definitely pushing it). They also had to give the impression of being pure—they had to be single.

The traditionalists still say that once a winner, you are expected to keep your beauty-queen appearance for life. Even if you are fifty-five and a grandmother, you still have to try to look the way you did when you were twenty-five.

Ex—beauty queens in their thirties and forties say this is keeping a lot of plastic surgeons prosperous and a lot of ex—beauty queens anorexic.

Sure, there are pageants for married women. But women in the South traditionally marry early. The married moms walking down those pageant aisles are usually still in their twenties.

But now Guy/Rex, those mavens of beauty pageants in El Paso, Texas, have created a beauty pageant that is setting New South women's hearts a-flutter.

"We call this pageant 'Over 35 and Fabulous!'" says Rex Holt. "It's the first pageant where more mature women have a chance. And the first pageant where homemakers can mix with career women."

It's going to be revolutionary in other ways as well: The contestants won't have to wear swimsuits. "Something to show the form," Rex says. "But not something that will make it obvious you aren't eighteen anymore."

"Yeeea," says thirty-nine-year-old Lurleen Paige of Columbia, South Carolina. "I've been in pageants since I was three, but I had to quit when I started to bulge just a bit in the stomach. My cousin did one of those mother-daughter beauty pageants where you compete together. But my cousin was forty-four and her daughter was nineteen. I wouldn't be caught dead on stage in a bathing suit next to a teenager."

Lurleen says beauty pageants are a tradition in the South and she doesn't see why they can't continue at all ages.

"I mean when you're staying in shape for a pageant," she says, "you keep yourself looking your very best. It's like a nice reminder to always have good posture and to never forget to wear your makeup. How nice of Guy/Rex to let us keep feeling competitive, even with a little cellulite."

Guy/Rex have always been pioneers. They don't think you should stop competing at any age. They say even if you're a grandmother and gorgeous, you should keep doing those chin exercises and stay toned. If you can still walk down a ramp, there'll soon be a pageant for you.

And recently, there have even been great strides in the most traditional of beauty pageants — the Miss America Pageant.

Southern women, who no longer feel winning the swimsuit competition is the height of the pageant experience, point out that Miss Alabama, Miss Tennessee and Miss Virginia are often more political these days than the presidential candidates.

The Miss America contestants now adopt a *platform* as part of their competition. Some might pick the environment. Others might tackle family abuse.

During the last presidential campaign, the contrast was stunning. None of the candidates seemed to want to commit to anything. The Miss America candidates, on the other hand, were holding all kinds of press conferences to talk about world affairs.

If you wanted to know something about Iran-Contra, you couldn't get it from the White House. You had to ask Miss Mississippi.

## Flying High at Fifty

Having to go out and find a job after getting a divorce is a social change that is certainly not confined to the South. But Southern women who were raised as belles have come up with some creative ways of starting all over at fifty.

A growing number of them are becoming flight attendants.

They say it's the perfect job for a woman who has spent her life being charming.

"My son almost fell over when I told him, at age forty-nine, I was applying to be a flight attendant," says Sherrill Sanders of Richmond, Virginia. "He said it was demeaning for me. Just two years before I had chaired an important charity event. What was I going to do when I ran into all those people who had been on my committee when they took my flight? Wouldn't I be embarrassed having to serve them?"

She said not nearly as embarrassed as they should be knowing that they have totally dropped her after the divorce in favor of the ex-husband and his new wife and all of his millions of dollars.

"It's the perfect job for me," says fifty-one-year-old Ellen Reiner of Jacksonville, Florida. "In fact, it might be the only job I qualify for that offers a little excitement. I've been a hostess all my life and I've catered to my husband's friends, so I'll also bring some maturity to the job. Airlines are hiring older women and I can't wait. I've applied to three companies. I'm in great health. I just know one of them will take me. I wanted to fly when I was nineteen, but I got married instead.

"My husband is now married to his secretary. I'm letting the kids, who are in college, live with them. I've got a small apartment and I'm going to fly."

Airline executives say they are delighted to hire older women.

One forty-eight-year-old woman said her ex-husband

was incredulous when he found out she was going to be a flight attendant.

"But you know, I think when he realized how much free flying I can do anywhere in the world, it might have been the first time he wanted to get back together. But I don't need him. I can go to Paris on my own, without his credit card."

"I applied when I became single again at the age of forty-seven after almost thirty years of marriage," says Susan Sadler Cox, now fifty-one, who flies for American. She wasn't the oldest trainee in her class.

She says she was definitely raised as a belle who never thought she'd have to be worrying about work at age fifty.

"I grew up in New Orleans, was an Ole Miss cheerleader, all of those things." She did have two degrees, but

*Flight attendants Vicki Campbell, left, and Susan Cox. Starting again at fifty.*

they did her no good. She had no work experience.

"I had a friend who was my age who was flying for American, and she encouraged me. I was scared to death during a lot of the training. I just wasn't sure I could do it. But I did and I'm having a wonderful time."

One fifty-three-year-old Columbus, Georgia, belle

who is now flying says she had a romantic dream of being a flight attendant when she was eighteen.

"That was back in the 'coffee, tea, or me' days when they were all girls and called stewardesses. You flew to meet an exciting man. But my mother wouldn't allow me to do that. She thought it was trashy and that I'd meet the wrong kind of men. Instead I married a man from back home with all the right social connections. The marriage was awful.

"I'm having a wonderful time, but at fifty-three, I don't think I'm going to meet the man of my dreams on an airplane. Things haven't changed that much. They're still looking for the cute twenty-year-olds."

Not necessarily.

Vicki Campbell was a flight attendant for American Airlines in her twenties. She's back after almost thirty years.

Her roommate during her new flight training was her daughter's age. Vicki had a successful career as an interior decorator, but went back to being a flight attendant because of the bad economy and because she just loves to fly.

Not only is she enjoying what she's doing. She also met her new husband on the job. He's a pilot.

Does she think it's different for women in the early nineties than it was for her as a flight attendant back in the early sixties?

"Definitely," she says, but then Vicki's a belle with some New South ideas. If she were in her twenties today, she'd train to be a pilot.

Some of the most traditional women in the South are even taking courses to learn to be mechanics and service their own cars. Truly something that could make Grandmother turn over in her grave.

But a car dealership in Montgomery is catering to those Old South traces that are still in the New South woman: They planned to teach a course to women in the fundamentals of car repair but realized they probably wouldn't attract certain women if the course was called "Know Your Engine."

*They* know their audience: The course is called "Glamour and Grease."

## Chapter Six

# Big Times, Big Deals, Big Hair

I keep reading all this stuff about Southern women and big hair. It's true, women around here have always liked to fluff up. But to think big hair is hiding small brains is ridiculous. And besides, I was in New York last month. Some of the women there have hair just as big or bigger than anyone in Texas or Mississippi. Just look at the East Coast society ladies they are always writing about in *W*. When they leave their hairdressers I'll bet there isn't a can of hair spray left in the entire state of New York. And what about those Beverly Hills women! They've got the biggest hair of all.

—An Alabama woman at a beauty make-over in Birmingham

## We Like Being Colorful

Southern women are not always happy about the way they are portrayed in the national media. Magazines tend to follow stereotypes when talking about belles from New Orleans and Montgomery.

"I guess it's because those magazines are put together in New York. They wear a lot of black in New York. But we don't. Things are more colorful down South," a woman from Georgia says. "You know if those beauty magazines were published in Atlanta or Memphis instead of New York, I bet we'd find there are things to laugh about in Manhattan, too, but we wouldn't do it, because we're too polite."

"I think it looks real pretty to wear floral prints in the summer. It goes with the weather," says a Tennessee belle. "Okay, so you don't see that on Fifth Avenue. But you know what you do see on Fifth Avenue? Sixty-year-old women wearing skirts so short they are just about a half inch away from indecency. They look ridiculous. In New York, women follow fashion trends no matter *what*."

"Silly and fluffy, without a thought in our heads, that's what those Northern women think we are," says Paula Kingsley of Mobile.

She says she doesn't mind good-natured kidding. Southern women like to laugh at themselves and they admit they like to dress up.

"But those magazines go too far. They actually had an

article last year that featured Southern women who do nothing more taxing than arrange flowers. They were also bragging that they never had to do anything so tacky as work for money. That story put being blonde on about the same level as being brain dead. That's about as accurate as saying everyone in New York is like Leona Helmsley.

"That writer also had the nerve to say that Southern women are redefining themselves in indelible ink. Ha!

"I am a woman with a very good job, three kids and a master's degree. I look good because I want to and I work hard because I want to. I don't know how it is in the North, but in the South, it's quite possible to do both. And as far as how we look, we look great. Southern women are as chic as women anywhere in the world."

But Andrea Fisher of New York doesn't agree.

"I watch these women move here from Nashville and Jackson and they just look overdone. They don't look put together. They're wearing so many bright colors they look like they should be on stage, dancing in a chorus line. For Southern women to do well here, they have to learn to dress better and be more chic."

New York fashion consultant Leon Hall says that's where Northern women make their mistake. They've been wearing nothing but black for so long, they can't get out of their own self-imposed dark tunnel. He says there's a whole wide world out there past Madison Avenue.

"Just about every second and third wife I know in New York is Southern," he says. "They're bright, sharp and intelligent. But they dress for their bodies, not their minds. That doesn't mean they don't have a mind. There is a difference."

Hall, who frequently talks fashion on such programs as "The Joan Rivers Show," says Southern women never plan a wardrobe around a simple black suit.

"They want clothes for every occasion. They understand color. They understand clothes for the right occasion. Bob Mackie ought to get down on his knees and thank God for the Southern woman. They love his glitter. They have the occasions to wear his ball gowns. I have never understood New York's passion for gray, brown and black. Nor do I understand designers putting leathers and suedes into their spring collections. Who the hell is going to wear it?"

## Sometimes We Just Light Up

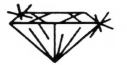

A New York woman who was in South Carolina last Christmas was amazed at how "eccentric" she felt the Southern women were dressing.

"They were wearing outfits that had lights on them that actually lit up," she explained. "No New York woman would walk down the street dressed like that."

The Southern woman she was talking to was amazed.

"Don't sweaters come with batteries in New York?"

"My God, no," said her Eastern friend. "Never. I can't imagine anyone in Bloomingdale's lit up like a Christmas tree."

But in the South, women who light up get only appreciative glances. Southern women love costume. They love glitz, they love glitter and they're not above putting on a few battery packs if the occasion calls for it. Flashing lights are reserved for Christmas outfits, however, and only if your sweater has a Christmas tree on it or your earrings are red-and-green wreaths. And okay, maybe a skirt that lights up on all the twelve days of Christmas. But everyone knows that lights are inappropriate on the Fourth of July. The Fourth of July is the time for rhinestones and sequins.

## The New South Look

Designer Richard Brooks has a great feel for designing for the Southern woman. He says this is because he was once practically a Southern belle himself.

"I was the first man to get a fashion degree at Louisiana State University," he says. "That was in the early sixties. The girls hated it because I was getting all the attention."

But it put him in close proximity to see how these young women felt about their clothes and how they looked.

It was also a golden time to be at LSU. Brooks was drum major for the band the year LSU had the number one football team in the country. He designed the costumes for the Golden Girls, the first dance troupe for the LSU band.

"And somewhere out there, there is a pledge from my

*Dress designer Richard Brooks learned about the Old South from the days when he was a high school drum major.*

*New South busy Governor Ann Richards makes sure her hem is straight.*
*Queen Elizabeth does not.*

fraternity who is probably in therapy today because I fitted my senior project outfit on him."

Brooks is now designing dresses out of Dallas. A large part of his clientele is Southern.

"But today, I design for the strong New South woman," he says. "These women have a mind of their own. They have careers and projects that take up a lot of time. Even the traditional society woman is dressing differently today. It's not just a matter of luncheons and balls anymore. Raising money for charities is getting tougher and tougher. They go into the boardrooms to get that money. They want to look attractive — but also strong and authoritative."

Among his clients is Governor Ann Richards of Texas, and he consulted on one of First Lady Hillary Clinton's inaugural gowns.

"These women don't have a lot of time to spend on fashion," he says. "I once fitted Governor Richards in a ladies' room at the Dallas–Fort Worth airport while a state trooper was standing guard outside."

These New South women have special needs. Not only do they have to look good for their personal lives, they also have to have clothes that won't look silly in the boardroom or aboard a corporate jet. No ruffles drooping in the soup. No overdone, flowery creations.

Detail is particularly important when the client is so often in the public eye.

Richard has a picture on his wall of Ann Richards in a white Richard Brooks ball gown. She is standing next to Queen Elizabeth, who is in a beige ball gown. The queen's hem is sagging and uneven. The governor's hem is perfectly straight.

"I used to design around social calendars," he says. "Now I design around itineraries. These women like colors and they want to look great—while maintaining authority."

Because his clients are so high profile, he is frequently asked what sizes these women are.

"All of my clients," he says, "are Richard Brooks size fours."

The designer says he enjoys creating clothes for New South women, but admits he remains an Old South man.

"In my family I'm the one who still clings to tradition." His wife, Judy, is in the financial end of the business. "She was not a Southern belle when I married her," he explains. "My mother wasn't sure how this would work out."

Mrs. Brooks says she didn't cook and she didn't iron shirts. She didn't care about the silver patterns. He did.

Their daughter, Catie, a student at Southern Methodist University, is definitely a woman of the New South. But her father is happy to say she still has a Southern sense of the dramatic.

For Christmas she decided she wanted a black full-length fake-mouton cape. With it she wears a pin that says 'Thank you for not killing animals.'"

Brooks says women are changing much faster than men in the South and admits he still has to get used to a woman paying for dinner or ordering the wine.

"But my wife and daughter have worked on me. I am very happy that they are the women they are. I'm very proud of them and let them know I realize this is a New South. Women open doors for themselves and they write their congressman."

His daughter gently calls him on that. "They write their congress*person*, Dad."

## The Boutique Ladies

These are not the women you'd expect to be clerking for just a little over minimum wage. Their children are in the best schools, their husbands are governors, mayors and CEOs, their closets are filled with designer outfits.

Many of them have never worked before. They don't even know their social security numbers. They have no reason to be standing on their feet all day.

But at Steinmart specialty discount stores all over the South, these women are what owner Jay Stein calls his "secret weapons."

For his special designer discount boutiques at the Steinmart stores, he's hiring saleswomen right off the social registers. These socialites are now going on waiting lists for the privilege of working one day at the discount boutiques. Being a boutique lady has become so chic that some of the women say getting on the boutique payroll is almost like going out for Kappa Kappa Gamma.

The concept has been encouraged by Stein, whose family started the Steinmart stores back in 1907 in Greenville, Mississippi.

"My father always said if you are going to have a store, you've got to do something different," says Stein. "We've always been a discount store."

Every year in Greenville, they'd have big sales with liquidation and overstocked merchandise from such stores as Saks Fifth Avenue. Women came all the way from Memphis to shop.

The Saks sale was such a big event that socialites in Greenville who had never had a need to work would come up to Stein and tell him, "This is all so exciting and so much fun, I just wish I could work here for one week a year." Then they'd go off and comb the sale for hidden bargains.

When the store was expanded to Memphis, Stein thought the concept might work on a permanent basis.

His idea was to hire local society women to work one day a week in the store's new designer boutique. Clothes and merchandise in other parts of the store is in a different price range. The boutique ladies are only assigned to the designer section.

The idea caught on fast. Women were recruited through friends and word of mouth. Now there are fifty stores and hardly anybody turns down an invitation to be a boutique lady. And since it's just one day a week, they can easily juggle the job between family, Junior League, charity ball committees and community volunteering.

"And," explains one woman, "there are also backup ladies who can be called on to substitute in case we might need to go off with our husbands. We're very close knit. We help each other out. It's like being in a sorority. Nobody ever quits, because we love it."

If a boutique lady needs six weeks off to go to Europe, no problem. There are plenty of fellow boutique sisters who are waiting to help out while she's gone.

Boutique ladies don't work nights and they don't work weekends.

Until recently, in the New Orleans store, they didn't even have to ring up the sale slips or punch the clock. Now a computer makes that necessary.

"But we had to learn it and we did," says Joyce de la Houssaye, who has been at the job for five years.

She became a boutique lady to give her something to do after her husband died.

"My friends would come up to me and say, 'Do you know that's a *discount* store?' I said, of course. I love it. I love putting the clothes together and helping the people who come in."

Today her friends flock to the store for the designer bargains.

"We all dress from the boutique now," she says. "I'm always calling friends and telling them what's just come in."

The boutique ladies put a lot of Southern charm into their sales program. Mrs. de la Houssaye brings flowers from her garden and serves coffee, as do all the other boutique

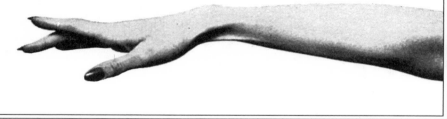

ladies. Last year she organized a storewide reception.

"The whole idea is to treat people here like we would in our homes," says another New Orleans boutique lady, Connie Killeen. She plans special events for the boutiques with every bit of dedication to detail as she would if she and the other boutique ladies were planning a private event for their own families.

But they say they are very serious about their work. For some, it's the first time they've ever made any money on their own. They are pleased they are so good at it.

Lana Bernos and Alma Weilbacher are the Wednesday boutique ladies at the New Orleans store. They admit they spend about what they make. But it's more than just the money and the selling. The women don't just bond with the designer discounts, they also bond with each other.

"It's kind of the Steinmart sorority," says one. "I feel very loyal and close to these people. And they make the atmosphere so much fun, it really *is* like being in a sorority."

The boutique ladies are given special luncheons and teas, and when they do something exceptional they are written up with *beaucoup* fanfare in the store's well-read newsletter.

Mrs. de la Houssaye was used to seeing her friends stop by to see if a new Perry Ellis or Oscar de la Renta had been shipped in, but she knew her discount boutique had arrived when one of the most social brides of the New Orleans season came in and wanted to be "put together."

"Now that girl could have bought anything anywhere that she wanted. She has that much money. But everyone likes a bargain."

There are waiting lists for the jobs at almost all the stores. One woman in Memphis explains she has high hopes of becoming "at least a substitute" sometime soon.

"It's the last place I would have thought I'd be looking for social acceptance," she says, "but it's a great concept. You stand on your feet a lot, but so what? And I'll tell you something, these days it's practical too.

"Money has been tight for everyone. A lot of our husbands are people you read about in the newspapers. But all businesses aren't doing so well. Being right there when the bargains roll in is going to save me some money. And that's a lot more than I can say for volunteering on a charity-ball committee."

## Chapter Seven

# The New Etiquette

> **R**ules, rules, rules. My grandmother in South Carolina had four sets of good china and rules for every occasion she was to use them. It was lovely, but it's from a time gone by. I don't worry about what's correct to serve and when. I don't have to. I work. My husband works. When we entertain, we use a caterer. I let her worry about the details. I just worry about the bill.
>
> —A woman from Charlotte, North Carolina, on entertaining in the New South

## iz Smith Is Not Ms. Smith in Mississippi (and Other Complexities of the New South)

There is no greater etiquette battle being fought in the South today than over the use of names.

In the Old South, it was easy. With Southern accents, everything came out sounding like Miz. You could be Miss or Mrs. and you were still called Miz.

It's a lot more complicated today now that political correctness has invaded the charity-ball committees. New South women who are being listed on charity committees as, say, Mrs. Jack Jones are incensed.

"I have a name of my own," says one woman. "I did the work, not my husband. I am Anne Jones."

"I want to be listed as Mrs. G. Donald Smith," says another. "I do this to honor my husband. I know he supports me. So I use his name to share in what I'm doing. Besides, that's the way we've always done it."

Her daughter is not at all supportive.

"You support Dad in the work that he does," says the daughter. "And he doesn't list himself as Mr. Janie Crawford. It doesn't have anything to do with being liberated. It has everything to do with having your own identity." She suggests if her mother wants to honor her father, she should take him out to dinner.

Older black women, on the other hand, prefer the social use of Mrs. George Robinson rather than Bernice Robinson.

"That's because servants were called by their first names and their employers were given their husband's names, which was considered more respectful," says one black woman. "I want to use my husband's name. It's a carryover. My daughter, however, is vehemently the other way. She doesn't care what went on before. She says this is now."

In small newspapers across the South, some society reporters are still using names like Mrs. Jack Smith as a byline. This column might be placed right next to a story written by a woman with a byline of Sherry Langford.

Some of their fellow journalists are horrified by the women who write under their husband's names, but the more old-fashioned columnists stand firm.

"There is a distinction," says a Mississippi woman who insists she always be listed on her column as Mrs. Horace Stanley. "If you're writing a story about an event where invitations were sent out, you can still use your husband's name. If you're one of the modern girls who are writing about murders and tarring the new roads—then you use your given name, period."

Martha McIntosh of Jackson, Mississippi, says the Jackson Junior League is a microcosm of how women have changed in the South.

"We used to be listed as Mrs. Mark F. McIntosh," she explains. "Then we progressed to Mrs. Mark F. McIntosh (Martha). Then we were just Martha McIntosh. Now it's Martha Stevens McIntosh (Mark)."

But formal invitations and charity committees in the South are still listing women by their husband's names.

"It's simply a matter of being correct," says Anne Simpson, a woman who plans parties in South Carolina. "That's what Amy Vanderbilt and Emily Post say is correct."

New South women just bristle at that. Then they delight in pointing out that it's *Emily* Post and *Amy* Vanderbilt.

Some women go to great lengths to prove their point. They refuse to join organizations unless they are listed as sponsors under their own names instead of their husband's names.

Dottie Griffith of Dallas found a very new solution to what she called a very Old South problem. When she became the patient of a chauvinist Southern dentist, she explained that she would be responsible for her own bill. The office insisted on having her husband's name.

When the bill was mailed, it was sent to the husband. The angry patient decided fair is fair. She sent her payment to the dentist's wife.

## Even Sir or Ma'am Is Not So Simple Anymore

While other Southern towns were battling it out with Ms., Mrs. and Miss, Houston has had a much more avant-garde name problem.

One of Houston's frequently photographed socialites, Kathryn McGuire, was a cross-dresser who always preferred to be identified as Ms. McGuire when she was pictured at social functions.

However, this wasn't the case during the day, when Ms. McGuire became Charles McGuire, owner of a Texas construction company. *His* employees called him "sir."

"We finally started identifying her as Charles/Kathryn," explains one newspaper writer. "That worked out best."

This was no joke. Charles/Kathryn burst onto the social scene at a time when Houston was at its lowest ebb financially. "Money was tight," admits one belle. "Anyone who could pay the price of a glitzy ball ticket could have the best table in the house. And Charles/Kathryn always went first-class in glittering designer gowns."

The *Houston Post* even named Kathryn one of the town's "Divine Divas" along with several others, including internationally known socialite Lynn Wyatt. The *Houston Chronical* has also featured Charles/Kathryn in its society pages, which prompted one reader to point out that Kathryn was wearing one leopard-skin outfit entirely too often.

Kathryn says she thinks her social attention was a lot more than just curiosity.

"At first maybe," she explains, showing a picture of herself in a navy designer suit with a very good label handbag. "But I am always careful to wear the best designer clothes and Houston respects that."

A divorced father of two, Charles/Kathryn says he was

always a cross-dresser. He finally had his name legally changed to Kathryn. Then people started calling him Ms.

He showed up at his construction office for an interview with a prospective employee in a designer gold blazer and blue high heels, which set off his long red hair.

Despite the clothes, the construction workers still think of him as a Mr.

"Don't forget you have a dress fitting this afternoon, sir," one of the employees called out. Kathryn says the seamstress, however, always uses "ma'am,"—that is, as long as Kathryn is fitting a dress.

Kathryn explains that the men at work had heard stories about his cross-dressing. So when he finally came to work as Kathryn, they weren't too surprised.

She does remember the day one particularly redneck customer came by looking for Charles and found Kathryn.

"I gave him a tough look and said, 'Do you have any

*Kathryn McGuire*
*in a society picture in the* **Houston Chronicle.**

© *Houston Chronicle,* 1989.

problems with my being dressed this way?' He looked at me for a minute and said, 'No sir.' "

She ran for Houston city council under the name Charles.

"I had to use Charles—that was my legal name then. I didn't do too bad; I came in second."

Recently Kathryn received a sex change.

"But despite all the publicity," she says, "the invitations have not stopped coming. They just see me as plain old Kathryn now. I've been around for quite a while."

Her supporters agree. Kathryn says if people were ousted because they were flaunting something that wasn't real, well, there just wouldn't be much left of high society.

## Frankly, My Dear, Does Anybody Give a Damn?

The Old South was filled with rules. The New South just keeps on breaking those rules.

The New South woman certainly doesn't check her watch the way her grandmother used to do.

The old rules had a lot to do with the clock.

"For one thing you never went to view a body at the mortuary before five o'clock in the afternoon," says one woman. "Now they're laying them out at eight o'clock in the morning. I called the funeral home to discuss this impropriety with them and they not-so-politely told me to mind my own business. Of course soon it's not going to matter anyway. I told my granddaughter how tacky I thought this was. She said it wasn't going to apply to her. She's going to be cremated."

It's not just funerals. Weddings, too, had their own rules.

In the Old South, everyone knew if a ceremony was at eight P.M. or after, that meant it was black tie. Not anymore.

Invitations come with the appropriate dress listed on the bottom.

"You've got to," says one woman. "They're getting married in all kinds of crazy places now. For all I know at eight o'clock these days they'll want you to come in cowboy clothes."

And then there is the question of jewelry.

In the Old South, one wore gold and silver jewelry during the day. No one would have dreamed of wearing diamonds before five P.M. In the New South, they wear diamonds to breakfast.

"And when you're writing about what's proper," one woman points out, "I'd like a good definitive call on the correctness of *winter white*."

She says she was brought up to never wear white shoes or outfits before Easter or after Labor Day. "Now even Nieman Marcus is touting *winter* white all year around.

"White is white," insists the woman. "I don't go for this nonsense about it being cream or ecru. I just don't feel right about seeing these young girls in white in December, even if the shoes are suede."

One longtime retailer who's an arbiter of Southern taste has always stood firm, despite fleeting fads and trends, but now he admits he's been forced to sell winter white in his store. *But* on the other hand, he has never been rigid. He's always been one to recognize change.

So when does he really think is the proper time to wear white shoes?

"Never," he says with conviction.

# Now What Was That Name Again?

When James Kramer married Cissy Cameron in a lovely South Carolina garden wedding, it certainly looked like a touch of the Old South.

The wisteria was in bloom. Dainty spun sugar love birds were perched atop a seven-tiered wedding cake. The eight bridesmaids all wore pastel chiffon with lace picture hats.

"We served honey-baked ham, biscuits, and the bride's cake was coconut with white frosting," explains Cissy. "That's traditional in my family. My grandmother is real Old South and she was so happy. I was glad because I haven't been a traditional, old-fashioned granddaughter. I lived with Jimmy for a year before we got married."

But all was forgiven when, dripping with Southern charm, she walked down the garden path.

The groom says the prenuptial year of living together was why they waited until after the wedding to tell his wife's grandmother about still another break with Southern tradition. Cissy was going to keep her maiden name.

The grandmother just smiled. Knowing her granddaughter all too well, she figured she would rebel at taking her new husband's name. The grandmother could live with that as long as James wasn't unhappy about it.

"I told her not at all," says James. "I'm from Wisconsin from a family that isn't very close. I don't even go home to visit. My mother is dead and my father is married to his third wife."

He told the grandmother he admired his new bride's attachment to her family. Getting to know them made him wish he had the same ties. That's when he decided to really turn the tables on convention.

Cissy didn't take his name. James went to court and took hers.

## Chapter Eight

# Sometimes I Think This Could Be Philadelphia

*I'm not against change, it's just that I'm afraid we're losing what's specially ours. Those new people are coming here with their new ideas and our kids are picking up things they see on television. It's not bad, it's just not what I'm used to. A lot of those new people try to pick up the old traditions and become one of us, but they give themselves away. I know if you're New or Old South by three things—your weddings, your closets and your bathrooms.*

—A traditional Southern belle's view of the New South

## There Are Dead Giveaways

Bella Carstairs subscribes to the old school of Southern belledom where your bosom can be fake but your pearls must be real. This Georgia grande dame claims she can watch a woman on television and tell if her pearls are real or not. But Bella admits it's a talent that is no longer in demand.

"My granddaughters don't even have real pearls. They don't want them. They prefer all this big, bulky, flashy jewelry. In my day, you were understated. It was elegant. It was proper.

"I realize pearls cost a lot of money these days. I thought maybe that was why the younger generation isn't going for them. But that's not the case at all. I almost fainted when I found out how much that fake jewelry costs. Whether you wear pearls or don't wear pearls has nothing to do with money. It's just new times and new tastes."

Bella puts the blame for Southern standards slipping squarely on the coming of air-conditioning.

"We stopped sitting on our porch swings in the

evening to keep cool and started staying inside to watch television. The kids started seeing things they wouldn't have ordinarily been exposed to. And then they started mimicking the accents they'd hear watching all that TV. Two generations from now, we're all going to sound alike.

"I remember when I was a girl, we thought everyone from California had been to college because they didn't talk with an accent. Now everybody talks that way."

Still another woman from Virginia says people are following fads. No one in the Old South followed fads. They followed their grandmothers. She sees all of the old times slipping away from births to weddings to funerals.

"I went to pay a call on a family in Richmond and they had the deceased laid out in the living room, kind of propped up in the coffin. In my part of Virginia, you would never do that. Propped up in the coffin indeed! I was so shocked, I almost forgot to leave my calling card.

"Then, not much later, I went to a funeral in Newport News and they had the casket open right out front in church. We never laid out the body anywhere but the funeral home. Now they just put them anywhere. It's all going to hell in a handbasket."

## Staying in the Closet in Texas

Closets have almost gotten out of hand in Texas. Women who grew up in historic old houses, where they needed an armoire just to have a place to hang their coat, are now building closets that are as big as some condominiums.

In fact, some of them *could* be condominiums. They have such accoutrements as chandeliers, refrigerators, telephones, chaise longues and several rooms that separate ball gowns from shoes from everyday wear. And of course there are rooms for winter *and* summer clothes.

The one element that is the same in all the New South closets is the automated rack that circles the room, just like in dry-cleaning establishments.

"I even have a massage table in my closet," says

Elaine Alden of Dallas. "I'm very busy. I have an investments business, three stepchildren and a lot of charity commitments. Clothes are extremely important to me. I have a master list of everything I own and I spend a lot of time in my closet. When we built this house, we built the closet to my specifications. It's like my own apartment. It's my getaway."

But it is Sharon McCutchin of Dallas who has the most famous closet of all.

This closet is so big that during the Republican Convention in Dallas in 1984, the rumor was she planned to give a dinner party for the *entire* Georgia delegation in her closet.

This was reported for days in the national media. A dinner party in a closet was considered very Texas and lots of TV stations wanted to cover the party live.

But as it turns out, the story was exaggerated.

Sharon didn't give the Georgia delegation a dinner party in her closet. That was ridiculous. It was only a cocktail reception.

## Putting on the Grits

Community cookbooks are a cherished part of the Old South heritage. Such organizations as the Junior League, the Junior Auxiliary, the Symphony League, the Arts Council, the church sisterhood, the sorority alumnus and the pilgrimage committee have all collected members' recipes and sold them as an annual fund-raiser.

The cookbooks have sold well and have been passed down through the generations. Collected for posterity are such Southern gems as "Aunt Pit's Banana Pudding," "Uncle Leroy's Coconut Crumble," "Betty's Company Spare Ribs.

And for most of these years, getting your recipes into these books was exceedingly political. In some cases, being included was as much a tribute to your popularity as your cooking skills. Sometimes it was best not to hurt anybody's feelings, so there would be six recipes for chicken casserole (Donna's Chicken Surprise, Martha's Sunday Chicken, Jeanie's Chicken Delight, and so on), all having exactly the same ingredients. And all coming right from the recipe on the back of the can of Campbell's Cream of Chicken soup.

There were also recipes from some of the best Southern cooks around.

These books have made millions of dollars, but they are changing with the times, just like everything else.

Now the organizations are not just going for folksy recipes that will sell in the next county or the next state—they want worldwide distribution. They've cut out the lard, cut out an overabundance of sugar and have hired national marketing research companies to determine just what will make these cookbooks sell in the Hampshires as well as in Hattiesburg.

"The biggest problem we had in changing our books," explains one cookbook coordinator, "was to stop putting people's names under the recipes. This had been done for years and it was a real vanity thing.

STIRRING RECIPES FROM MEMPHIS

HEART&SOUL

THE JUNIOR LEAGUE OF MEMPHIS, INC.

"There were tears and fights and threats of quitting the club from some people. But in the end, it's worked out so much better. No one knows whose recipes were finally chosen except a few people on the final committee. It's really funny, some of the worst cooks—the ones who always submitted canned-soup casseroles—are now going around claiming to be the contributors of the best recipes. But so what? If that's what it takes to keep everyone happy, great. We've got a much better cookbook because of it."

The new Southern community cookbooks are even being taken seriously in places like Oregon and Illinois. But what has made the best ones so successful is that they have managed to combine the tradition of the old with very special touches of the new.

The Jackson, Mississippi, Junior League cookbook, *Come On In!*, is slick and innovative and has gotten rave reviews in such places as the *New York Times* and the *Detroit News*. But despite its nouvelle touches, it never loses sight of the fact that it's a Southern cookbook.

*Come On In!* has doorways as its theme.

"Here in the South, doors symbolize our famous gift for hospitality, a legend which happens to be true. In earlier days the hospitality began even before you reached the door; in today's air-conditioned South, if a house has any sort of front porch at all, it's usually a token gesture at best." So this book features doors and entranceways that go along with each recipe section from the imposing entranceway of an antebellum mansion to the squeaky door of a screened porch leading to a kitchen.

There is not a canned-soup recipe to be found.

The Memphis Junior League also wanted a national, even international, audience for its new cookbook.

"So we hired a marketing research firm to find out just what would make our book marketable everywhere," explains Lisa Colcoloough, cookbook cochair. "It's very important because this cookbook will fund most of our community projects."

The research showed that outsiders think of music as well as good food when they think of Memphis. The result is a recipe collection called *Heart & Soul.*

"It celebrates all the ethnic diversity that we have in Memphis as well as saluting all the music legends from W. C. Handy to Elvis Presley."

No members' names appear under these recipes either.

Instead, everyone who participated is listed in the acknowledgments by her *own* name, not her husband's.

Lisa explains they've taken the cookbook to several gift shows and have served food samples from the book, including an appetizer called Dixie Caviar that features black-eyed peas and hominy.

"We'd get people stopping by from places like Iowa and Oregon and they were very wary of hominy. They thought it might be something like animal parts. We'd explain it's just corn. They really liked the dish. They just weren't used to some of our Southern delicacies. It's been fun exposing our food and culture to new people."

The cookbook has a section devoted to Elvis, and a party to celebrate the book's publication was held at Graceland.

A major sign to some that times have indeed changed.

"We couldn't even have Elvis records in our house when I was growing up. Now they have our cookbook party at Graceland," says one attendant. "Personally, I'm delighted. It gave me an excuse to go and I loved it. Who would have thought when Elvis was alive that the Junior League would be partying at Graceland?"

## You Can Always Tell

Much about the Old South and New South is so blended together that it's hard to tell which is which. But still, no matter how much money you have, how much coaching you have and how many sponsors you have, there are ten ways you can always tell that you're new money in the Old South.

1. Your plastic surgeon buys an entire table at the charity ball you're chairing.

2. Your bathroom is bigger than the town you were born in.

3. Your silver pattern wasn't inherited from your grandmother, it was recommended by your hairdresser.

4. The newer your money, the smaller the vegetables you serve at your dinner parties.

5. Your paintings match the sofa.

6. When people talk about you, they know how much money your house cost rather than who your grandfather was.

7. No little pearl earrings from Grandmother; your earrings are big enough to double as barbells in your aerobics class.

8. You've never heard of home-made cheese straws; your specialty is the miniature frozen quiches from Sam's.

9. You don't have a file of family recipes, you have a file of caterers.

10. Your pearls are fake. But your money is real.

# The New South Weddings

Old South weddings were always traditional, from the cream-colored engraved invitations to the frosted white wedding cake. Brides wore white and the brides-maids matched the punch.

These kinds of weddings were the Old South. But in the New South, there is often as much pageantry at a wedding as there is at a Mardi Gras ball.

In New Orleans they are *still* talking about the 1985 wedding Mickey Easterling put on for her daughter Nancy.

"I know of one person that tried to duplicate it," Mickey says, "but they couldn't do it."

The reception was at the New Orleans Museum of Art. There were three bands. *One* of them was the New Orleans Symphony.

Eight hundred guests dined on filet mignon, smoked salmon and caviar. The grand ball was covered in vines, flowers and lights. Limousines circled the parking lot to pick up guests and deliver them in style to the front door. It just seemed more festive than ordinary valet parking.

A special attraction at the end of the evening was a fireworks display across the lagoon that lit up the sky with the names of the bride and groom—Nancy and Fred—with swans and rings intertwined.

Mickey explains that while she's from New Orleans, she still has some very New South ideas. She delights in being unconventional. Her trademark is hats and she wears one for every occasion.

Her lavish and inventive entertainments are always dis-cussed. She once rented a villa in Morocco and invited friends from all over the world to visit, one at a time.

In New Orleans, she gives parties in conjunction with a fund-raiser for visiting celebrities such as Lena Horne. For that particular party, she built a grape arbor and served supper in Saks Fifth Avenue dress boxes.

Mickey even shows flair in her oversized bathroom, which has a refrigerator that is stocked with champagne at all times. Among the furnishings are antique chairs.

Mickey is divorced and says she is an independent

woman who manages her own business affairs. What is her business?

"Everyone wants to know that," she says, lifting her perfectly arched brows, "but I prefer to keep some things a mystery."

She delights in being flamboyant.

"I have the largest collection of Zandra Rhodes dresses of anyone," she says. Her art can also be avant-garde. She has a collection of nude paintings on the third floor of her home.

She smiles when she recalls that the day after her daughter's wedding they had a "going away" luncheon for the bride and groom at Galloitoires restaurant. This is an old-guard restaurant in New Orleans that never takes reservations. Galloitoires' one bow to the New South is that they recently started taking credit cards.

Mickey had her friends hold places in line so her guests wouldn't have to wait so long for tables. Meanwhile, she slipped in the back door and put champagne on all the empty tables and sent bottles to customers at other tables. No one blatantly breaks the rules at Galloitoires.

"It was the scandal of the city," she laughs.

It was a glittering wedding weekend and the parties for the bride and groom continued for several months after. Unfortunately, the wedding festivities lasted almost longer than the marriage.

"Her second marriage didn't last, either," Mickey recalls.

Was that wedding as elaborate as the first? This question quickly brings out the Old South in her.

"Well, of course not," she says. "That would be rather tacky, wouldn't it?"

In the old days, Southern weddings were often celebrated for several days because friends and relatives had come from all parts of the country and other friends and relatives would want to wine and dine them. Southerners have always been famous for their hospitality.

But Lillie Fontenot of Houston gave a very New South twist to this and just had her daughter's wedding last all day.

Monica Fontenot Poindexter is Lillie's only daughter and she wanted to make her wedding something magical and special. So instead of just having a typical reception, Monica's was a white-tie-and-tails wedding ball.

"We started with the wedding at ten A.M., followed by a brunch," says Lillie. "Then there was a small supper for the bridal party followed by a cocktail reception for all the guests at the Warwick Hotel so everyone could say hello to Monica and see her dress up close."

Then the ballroom doors were opened and the ball began. For entertainment, a cellist played, ballerinas danced and two opera singers performed arias.

*Mickey Easterling at her daughter's much talked about New South wedding.*

"I wanted this to be formal and I meant formal," she explains. Her husband, Louis Fontenot, a civil engineer who is in business for himself, agreed.

"I sent out letters along with the invitations," she said, "explaining just what white tie and tails meant. The

*The ladies' lounge of the Atlanta Fox Theater.* © Atlanta Landmarks Inc.

women's dresses were to be long, not more than an inch and a half from the floor. I was very specific."

She says the men took her instructions to heart. They all came in white tie and tails.

"But some of the women thought they could get away with shorter dresses. They didn't. The ones that weren't dressed properly went home."

Weddings aren't the only way to immediately pick out new customs. Bathrooms, too, seem to take on new personalities in the New South.

Jana Everson found a way of combining both.

"My mother was born in Atlanta," she explains. "She is about as much of a Southern belle as you can get. I now live in Mississippi, but when it was time for my wedding, I wanted to have it in Atlanta."

She was looking for something with Old South style and yet a new twist.

"I found the perfect thing," she says. "My mother grew up going to the Fox Theater, a real Atlanta landmark. It is an incredible place. It looks like an Egyptian palace. Even the bathrooms are more elaborate than most real-life palaces."

Like many of the old movie houses, the Fox Theater has closed down but is still available for special events. In fact, it can be rented out for most occasions.

"I knew the place I wanted to have my wedding was the Fox Theater," she says. "I just didn't know which part of it. Then after walking through, I knew exactly where — in the ladies' bathroom. Well, it's really the ladies' lounge, because it's so big with so much wonderful decor."

She thought the people in charge of the Fox would think she was crazy, but not at all. They said the ladies' lounge had been used for weddings many times.

"It was an elegant occasion," she says. "And the pictures from it are wonderful. People always ask where I found such an exotic setting. You should see their jaws drop when I tell them it's a ladies' bathroom."

Chapter Nine

# The Torch Is Passed

*I* went to school in California, got a master's degree and really expected to stay in California. But I grew up in Nashville, all my ties are in Nashville, and the more I was away, the more I missed home. Coming back hasn't been without its problems. I'm very liberated. My mother is trying hard to understand this. She's proud of me, but a little defensive. I hear she always discusses me by saying, "We're so proud of Donna, she's working in a hospital with children and doing so well. She's not married, you know. But the girls are marrying later these days— I'm sure there's still plenty of time."

—A Nashville woman on being a woman of the New South and still pleasing your mother

101

## My Daughter's Not a Ball Chairman, She's a Rotarian

The New South woman still volunteers like her mother, but she has different goals. Her mother tried to understand when her daughter didn't make her debut and went to graduate school instead. But the daughter could have made it all up if she had just come home and got on the invitations committee for the Magnolia Charity Ball. But something terrible happened to her in graduate school. Once she got her degree, she turned down an invitation to join the Junior Auxiliary. All she wanted to talk about was five-year plans and venture capital.

And then came the real blow. She had no intention of getting involved in something like the art museum gala.

She wanted to do something more meaningful. She was joining the Rotary Club. She'd meet better business contacts.

"What about giving your time to the community?" a mother chastised her daughter. "Those balls aren't just social. They raise a lot of money for good causes."

But, more and more, the daughters are giving money to the charities and using their time to get on with their careers.

And when they do volunteer, they like to take on projects where their husbands will be working with them.

No silly etiquette about the listing of names here. Both are listed by their own names—even if the last name is, more often than not, his.

"Not that it really makes a difference," one young woman explains. "I mean I'm not rigid like my mother has always been. But on the program, we *should* be listed as Jane and Sam Logan, not Sam and Jane Logan. Of course no one's really uptight about this. But proper is proper and there ought to be *some* standards."

Traditionally, Southern volunteer groups met during the day. Now so many women are working that most organizations also have meetings at night for the career women.

"I'm from a little town in Mississippi," says one woman. "I made my debut, did the whole bit. I went to school at Vanderbilt and now I'm a stockbroker. My mother barely lifted an eyebrow when I kept my own name. She didn't say a word when I had a baby and went back to work after two months. But when I joined the Toastmaster's Club she was aghast."

"That was a club your father was in," her mother explains. "It was always for men. They sat around and smoked cigars. You are a beautiful young girl. That's not a club for girls!"

"My mother thinks I work too hard. She wants me to join clubs that have parties where I can wear pretty dresses. I told her I need business contacts. I can't get those in the garden club."

Her mother just will not adjust.

"No wonder," she keeps telling her daughter, "I go to charity balls these days and see they're all being run by girls who came here from places like Illinois. Wait until your grandmother [in Virginia] hears about this."

The grandmother wasn't as upset as expected, however. She had some news of her own. She and her husband had sold the family home and bought a Winnebago. They're traveling from Virginia to California.

Betsy Parish is a New South belle who would surely have shocked her grandfather. She is the first woman in her family to be salaried.

The Parishes' ties in the South go back for generations. They have always been considered *lovely* people who did nothing excessive or flashy in public. No Parish was ever written about in newspapers except for the most discreet social affairs. A tasteful obituary was, of course, acceptable.

That's the Old South. Betsy is very much a woman of *today*. She's had a successful career in public relations. She has not only been in the newspapers, she now writes a gossip column for the *Houston Post*.

Her beat is the Houston *boldface* society—these are the flashy, glitzy Texans whose names she lists in boldface type. A practice her grandfather could not possibly have conceived of.

The Parish family was once mentioned in a newspaper column back in 1956. Betsy's uncle Bob Parish was in New York City at the time and he was an item in the then-powerful Dorothy Kilgallen's column. Her grandfather was not amused.

"Oil heir Bob Parish," Miss Kilgallen wrote, "planed in from Texas the minute he learned the dazzling blonde Connie Towers was in town. His pop is the chairman of the Houston Gas and Light."

Letters were quietly written to the grandfather from friends telling him they had read this shocking item.

Betsy's grandfather felt it was necessary to write to a friend in Shreveport and comment on this breech of Southern etiquette.

"You and I," he wrote, "have the satisfaction, solace, consolation and joy of knowing that in spite of all of our individual and joint years in New York, and the thousands of opportunities we had to do something that would put us in the newspaper columns, we never made it. I believe we can rest on that indisputable record."

## Five Things an Old South Mother Feels the Need to Explain About Her New South Daughter

1. She's not married because she's trying to get her money's worth out of that $100,000 education her parents so generously provided her.

2. She's applied to be a Rhodes scholar. After Oxford, she'll have more time for a lovely wedding.

3. She's not married because she went to school up North. When she comes home, she'll settle down and have a lovely wedding.

4. She's not married because she's waiting until she's finished her medical internship. It's so hard to plan a lovely wedding when you're on a surgical rotation.

5. She's only thirty-five. Girls are getting married later these days. Lots of girls over thirty-five are settling down and having lovely weddings.

# The Rules Changed in the Middle

The Brennan name is now as much a part of New Orleans tradition as Mardi Gras and creole gumbo.

But Cindy and Lally Brennan and Ti Brennan Martin are the new generation. They are proud of their Southern roots, but are constantly breaking new ground.

The three are cousins, all in their thirties.

"We were raised when there was only *one* set of rules," says Cindy. "And somewhere along the way, all the rules started changing."

Their family restaurants are among the most popular in the city. But the original Brennan brothers and sisters know all too well what a hard, tough life it is running a food establishment.

Even when you've got such successes as Commander's Palace and Brennan's, the hours are long and the days off are few.

"So they encouraged us kids to go off and be what-ever we wanted," says Ti. "They just told us not to be in the restaurant business. You don't have a life. Do anything but this."

Almost all of their thirteen cousins have gone into the restaurant business.

"Yes, we're New South," says Ti. "The boys went to Europe to learn to cook. The girls are into the financial end."

The cousins are all active in the restaurants. Lally helps operate Commander's Palace. Cindy, along with her brother Ralph, runs Mr. B's and Bacco's. Ti, with her cousins Brad, Lauren and Dick Jr. run the Palace Cafe.

"When we were kids," says Lally, "we had these Southern-belle, antebellum dresses. On holidays our parents would dress us up in those clothes and we'd go to the restaurants and hand out carnations. We'd try to rebel and say, '*Oh no*, it's Easter we're going to have to dress up.' We'd complain and moan, but when we got there, we loved it."

Cindy, Lally and Ti are in a unique position to view the changes in Southern lifestyles. People who used to entertain lavishly in their own homes just don't have the help they used to have. The Old South customers are now entertaining more and more in restaurants along with the new people whose traditions started two weeks ago.

Ti says even the most modern Southern women have retained a part of their heritage. It's like osmosis. It just seeps through.

Lally explains they can't possibly know all their customers like their parents once did. But still, they can always tell when someone's planning a party who is a real Southerner—and when they're from somewhere else.

"The Northern women will usually fax me instructions," says Ti. "The Southern women come in person. They measure the table, give instructions on how to place the napkins and explain *exactly* where the flowers will go. The waiters don't always understand, but I tell them they don't know how these ladies used to entertain in their homes. This is all minor compared to that."

Even for a party at a restaurant as well known for food as the Brennan establishments, the Southern women still have to feel they are a part of the food preparations.

"They bring their own cheese straws or some other little tidbit they've done themselves," says Lally. They bring their own silver candy dishes. They bring their own table decorations even if it's just for a small birthday lunch for two or three close friends.

"We understand that," says Cindy. "We were raised that way. There are just little touches you never forget."

They say even the most liberated of Southern women still hand their lipsticks to their husbands or boyfriends to hold when the women don't want to carry pocketbooks.

"The Northern men don't carry those lipsticks. They wouldn't even consider it."

The Brennan women have always worked. They've also always liked to look good. The cousins recall an aunt who always had lovely cigarette holders.

"And she always smoked Eve cigarettes," Lally explains. "She didn't particularly like that cigarette, but it was the prettiest one. It looked the best and she smoked that."

The cousins see themselves as very New South, but even when you're New South, you still hang on to a lot of the Old.

"Some of the new people just don't understand that. But the more they're here, the more they come around," says Ti. She recalls that a new friend who was not Southern was in the hospital with what could have been a serious illness. Family and friends from the North gathered around. But as soon as it was announced she was going to be okay, everyone left.

"I couldn't believe it," says Ti. "In the South, we stay until the person leaves the hospital. You don't leave people just because they're not as sick as you thought they were. Sometimes it's almost like a party. But your friends and family rally around."

The cousins laugh remembering a few months ago when Cindy had her baby. "We were all there with food and drinks," says Lally. "And the celebration went on right through the labor."

Cindy explains that her doctor had just started to take his own kids to see *Home Alone II* when she first got her labor pains. He had promised Lally he'd be with her, so he dropped the kids off and went to the hospital. She was told his kids were very disappointed. It had been planned as a big family outing.

Her cousins say Cindy responded as a proper Southern woman should.

"As soon as I could get out," Cindy says, "I bought a *Home Alone* video and a big pizza and delivered it to the doctor. I told him I couldn't fully make up for his missed day with his kids, but maybe that would help."

The cousins say they are very untraditional Southern women when it comes to a major New Orleans event, Mardi Gras. They've always loved riding on floats and don't care much about going to the balls.

"It's usually the other way around," says Cindy.

This year they've been told the title of their float will be "Someday My Prince Will Come."

"We hooted and hollered over that," says Ti. "We're not the kind of women who sit around waiting for our prince to come."

But they're still going to ride on the float. It's a lot of fun, and besides, they've been told that if they want to, they can dress like the prince.

*The new generation of Brennans — Cindy Brennan and Ti Brennan Martin.*
© Rosemary Carroll Butler

## Chapter Ten

# William Faulkner and Elvis Presley Loved It Here—And You Will Too

*I*'m sick and tired of hearing all those Northerners complain when they arrive that they're sure they'll never have an intellectual conversation away from the bright lights of New York City. What do they think, that Tennessee Williams was born in Brooklyn?

—A Louisiana woman on Northern transplants

New people are moving to the South in droves— some kicking and screaming because they've been transferred by their companies. Give them a year and they become more Southern than the Southerners. But they sometimes refuse to believe they can even live here when they first find out they have to leave Chicago or Los Angeles or Boston.

They've never been South and they don't know what life is like in "the provinces."

Will they ever eat another decent gourmet meal? Will they ever see another decent play? Will they ever experience real culture again?

"I moved to Jackson, Mississippi, from Philadelphia," says Jan Carmichael. "The first time some of my relatives were to come down to visit, they were having a fit. They couldn't imagine what we'd have here in Jackson to keep them entertained.

"Well, right off they were charmed by all the hospitality of my new Southern friends. But my cousin Donald still wasn't convinced that he could take this place culturally. He saw an ad for a ballet competition and was very condescending. He thought it might be something like a ballet recital.

"I explained this was the International Ballet Competition. It rotates among only four places in the whole world—Varna, Bulgaria; Helsinki, Finland; Moscow, Russia; *and Jackson, Mississippi.*

"And if you were attending in Moscow, it wouldn't be as much fun because you wouldn't get to eat catfish and fried dill pickles."

Some people take a little more convincing. Charles Higgins threatened a lawsuit to try to keep from being moved to Dallas from New York when his company decided to transfer him. Much to his horror, it did no good.

"I thought I was going to die from culture shock," he admits. "My friends gave me a good-bye party and wore black armbands. At that point, I would have believed anything. I even considered carrying a Christmas tree on the top of my van when I drove to my new home. Someone told me you couldn't get a decent tree anywhere in Texas.

Was he ever surprised.

"I found trees in every possible texture and color from natural pine to hot-pink sequins," he says. "The green sequined cactus ornaments were a little strange, but I've learned a big lesson: Bloomingdale's doesn't carry everything."

The Texas newcomer also admits he anticipated another big problem with the South. He just didn't believe there could possibly be a decent museum, sym-phony orchestra or ballet company within miles of a region that practically has made a religion out of something called chicken-fried steak.

"There are fabulous museums in the South," he was told. "You know the King Tut and Catherine the Great exhibits didn't originate in New York or Chicago. They opened in Memphis."

Somehow he just wasn't listening.

This was in 1987. Higgins wasn't in Dallas for more than three months when a Russian ballet dancer defected at the transplanted New Yorker's neighborhood Tom Thumb grocery store. Andrei Ustinov of the Moscow Ballet leapt across the expressway, bounded through a parking lot and turned himself in to a Texas beauty who had just gone through the checkout line. They walked to an outside pay phone and called the FBI.

His new Texas friends ruthlessly chided Mr. Higgins about this incident. Talk about cultural deprivation. Not one of these Texans, it seems, could ever remember any *artiste* defecting at Zabar's in New York City.

# They're Celebrating Bar Mitzvahs at Graceland

If you're going to be in Tennessee, sooner or later all roads lead to Graceland. Now you can do more than just tour the mansion. You can also have a party on Graceland property.

Brides are reserving it for their rehearsal dinners. International corporations are using it for sales conferences. It has even been the scene of some Bar Mitzvah celebrations.

"Now you can't have the parties in the mansion," explains an official. "They're just held on Graceland property. But we do offer special private night tours as part of the package."

Graceland caters. You can have a black-tie, prime-rib dinner. Or you can order some of Elvis's favorite barbecue.

"It's getting to be popular for Memphis people to have parties there as well as out-of-towners," says one Memphis socialite. "A lot of us have never been there, because it just wasn't exactly socially acceptable when we were kids. Now we're all dying for an excuse to get inside."

The Graceland people will provide any kind of musical entertainment the party givers wish.

There is only one stipulation. No Elvis imitators. This is the original Graceland and only the original Elvis is king.

Graceland is preserved the way Elvis always wanted it. They explain no impostor is going to be brought in and make it tacky.

## Seductive Savannah

Savannah, Georgia, is a city that oozes Old South charm, with tree-lined squares surrounded by graceful antebellum town houses.

Newcomers are enchanted. Some explain they've come on vacation and have become so enamored that they end up going back home, packing up and moving to Savannah for good.

Sara Connors, formerly of Illinois, moved to Savannah two years after visiting for two days during a vacation tour of the South.

"*Gone With the Wind* was my favorite book," she explains. "I may have a Chicago accent, but in my heart I've always been Scarlett. I wanted to relocate near a beach. When I saw Savannah, it fulfilled all my dreams. I found a job and I moved. Of course Scarlett never had to be a secretary and I rented an apartment that's not exactly in Old Savannah because it's all I can afford. But it's a lot closer to my ideal than if I was in Chicago—and the weather is definitely better."

Japanese tourists also make pilgrimages to Savannah, Georgia, where they can trace the steps of Scarlett O'Hara.

One such group was staying at the city's Gastonian Inn when their leader asked the innkeepers, Hugh and Roberta Lindberger, for a special favor.

"They had read that one of Scarlett's favorite dishes when she came to Savannah was tapioca pudding," says Roberta. "They asked if I could fix this delicacy."

She did and the Japanese visitors sat around eating the pudding with an almost religious reverence.

These were publishers who were going to print the Japanese-language version of *Scarlett* (Alexandra Ripley's sequel to *Gone With the Wind*). Roberta says they told her the people of Japan are fascinated by the American South. There was no detail of Scarlett's life they found too trivial to pursue.

Roberta and Hugh are pretty intrigued with the

South themselves. They came to Savannah from California for a brief vacation. They fell in love with the city's historic charm and, within days, had purchased two antebellum town houses and decided to become innkeepers.

But buying an Old Savannah home is one thing. Becoming a part of Old Savannah is quite another.

The Lindbergers are warm and outgoing and are popular with their guests. Roberta explains that they became involved in many civic and cultural endeavors when they opened the inn. This was much appreciated by the townspeople. But neighbors were worried about what a retail establishment would do to their street. Sure, there were doctors and lawyers who had their offices in their homes just a few doors down. But that was different. The Lindbergers weren't from Savannah. The neighbors weren't sure what all those outsiders coming and going would do to their street. They brought up ordinance after ordinance to try to keep the Lindbergers from succeeding.

"It was our stubbornness and perseverance that got us through all the stumbling blocks," Hugh explains.

He's quite genial about it and holds no grudges.

The couple have restored the inn (in two buildings) with careful historic detail (except for the oversized Jacuzzi tubs in all the historic bathrooms). This won most of their neighbors' respect and even precipitated a public apology from one. Though another still doesn't speak to them.

Now, even townspeople come and stay at the Gastonian to celebrate special occasions. Roberta says she loves Savannah and has made a lot of friends, but many are transplants like herself.

"We've been in a lot of the Old Savannah homes," she says. "But it's almost always for a civic or cultural occasion, something I've had to pay money to attend. In eight years, I can count on my fingers the times we've been invited to a private Old Savannah home for a purely social evening."

Roberta says she's patient. She's learning the Southern ways and knows that even in the New South, old ways take a long time to change.

Her husband says he doesn't know what she's talking about. He thinks they have been accepted everywhere. They've even been asked to join the First City Club, which has a lot of people from *new Savannah*.

But Roberta says they would never be asked to join one of the really Old Savannah institutions.

"Oh, we were asked to join one of those other clubs," says Hugh.

"Which one? Why didn't you tell me!" a completely flustered Roberta responds.

Hugh just looks puzzled. He says he didn't think it mattered. They were already in a club they liked. Roberta raises her eyebrows. Men who grew up in the Midwest just don't understand such things.

*The Gastonian Inn, an Old South home run by some New South people.*

## Yes, Tuscaloosa Has a Yacht Club and More Than a Few Georgia O'Keeffes

Jack Warner built a yacht club in Tuscaloosa, Alabama. It's quite a showcase. The only problem is, Tuscaloosa is in northern Alabama. Far inland and far away from any real water.

It doesn't matter. Warner has put his neobaroque yacht club on man-made Lake Tuscaloosa and filled it with priceless art.

He's also built a golf club that's modeled after a Chinese temple. This too is filled with art treasures.

"That's Jack," friends say as they roll their eyes affectionately. "Wait until you see what he's done with his paper company. Now, that's an art collection."

That's an understatement.

Warner is head of Gulf State Paper Corporation. His national headquarters houses one of the most extensive collections of American art anywhere in the world.

Like his yacht and golf clubs, this building is just not what you'd expect to see in a town in Alabama. The paper company building is red, in Japanese style and was inspired by the imperial palace in Kyoto (complete with a pool and rock garden in the central court). It's also surrounded by acres of Japanese gardens with contrasting ponds, waterfalls, shapes, textures and designs. Peacocks and other exotic birds wander throughout.

You could as easily think you were in Tokyo as Tuscaloosa. But just a few miles away, students are hurrying to class at the University of Alabama.

Art is everywhere in the Gulf State Paper Company offices. It's like a museum. Secretaries look through glass walls and gaze at paintings by Georgia O'Keeffe, Edward Hopper, Albert Bierstadt, Frederic Remington,

George Catlin and Andrew Wyeth, to name only a few.

"I'm an artoholic," Warner admits. "I am passionate about all of this."

First-time visitors are in awe. "Do people in other parts of the world know about this?"

"The National Gallery has sent a wish list," he says. He hears from most of the other major American museums too.

"But my collection is staying in the South," he explains.

Jack Warner started collecting Audubon prints right after World War II. Then he inherited three European paintings, which he sold, and bought some American ones.

What came next is a staggering array of American art from the nineteenth and twentieth centuries. Walk around and you'll see Sargents, you'll see Cassatts. Workers may pass by with their lunch bags, but their desks and offices are kept immaculate.

"The tours come through at the close of the day," one

*Jack Warner and some of his art collection.*

*The Gulf State Paper Company headquarters in Tuscaloosa, Alabama.*

woman explains. "This place is very beautiful. Mr. Warner expects us to keep it that way." As soon as the word processors are turned off, the tours begin.

Warner says he had his building designed with an Asian influence because he became infatuated with Far Eastern design during World War II, when he was in Burma.

He also saw a lovely old Southern home in the historic district of Tuscaloosa getting run down so he bought it, renamed it the Mildred Warner House, after his mother, and filled *it* with even more art.

Warner loves it when people think of him as eccentric. He always has tongues wagging around Tuscaloosa.

But he's lived in Tuscaloosa since he was a child. He's now in his seventies and no matter how extensive his financial interests or how important his art, he intends to stay there. World-famous people come to Alabama to visit him.

Lord Mountbatten once flew in on Warner's own jet. "I had the Tuscaloosa high school band playing for him when he stepped off the plane," says the paper company executive.

Warner's also a major University of Alabama football fan. In the midst of all the priceless art, his pet parrot, Bama, often wanders freely.

Visitors *ooh* and *aah* over the art as Bama whistles the Crimson Tide fight song.

## Down Here, Eccentricity Is a Virtue

The New South is a study in contrasts. In just one hour you can drive from William Faulkner's grave (Oxford, Mississippi) to Elvis Presley's grave (Memphis, Tennessee). What makes it so much fun is there are an awful lot of people who feel perfectly at home in both worlds.

This sometimes confuses people who live in other places. They don't understand that Southerners have always had a great tolerance for eccentricity. They not only accept it, they revel in it.

For one thing, Southern grocery stores have colorful names. But it's often a shock for someone moving in from Peoria to find their neighborhood supermarket has a name like the Piggly Wiggly or the Jitney Jungle.

"When my neighbor first told me to run down to the Piggly Wiggly and I'd find everything I need, I broke out in a cold sweat," one Georgia newcomer explains. "I was in Atlanta looking around for houses. My wife and I were going to move there. I always thought the city was extremely progressive. But how progressive can you be if the grocery stores are named Piggly Wiggly?"

Actually, Piggly Wiggly was named in 1916 by its founder, Clarence Saunders of Memphis. He never would explain just why he decided on that name. He'd just smile and say it was a name that got a lot of attention.

But this was no small-town country enterprise. Piggly Wiggly was the first grocery store in the country to be self-service. Mr. Saunders was also the first to provide checkout stands, the first to price-mark every item in the store and the first to use refrigerated cases for produce.

He was a man ahead of his time, and he never stopped being eccentric. In 1937, he tried still another concept. This time it was a fully automated store that he called the "Keedozzle" (for "key does all"). Mechanical failures, however, eventually closed the store.

The Jitney Jungle stores have a home office in Jackson, Mississippi.

They too are constantly getting calls about their name.

"The stores opened back in the 1920s," explains an employee. "*Jitney* was a slang term for a nickel. The name was supposed to be Jitney *Jingle,* which meant you could get more jingle out of your nickel. But there was a mistake in the newspaper ad and it came out Jitney Jungle. The customers liked that name better, so that's what it is."

These kind of Southernisms have been around for a long time. No one would dream of coming up with a more 1990s kind of name that would seem more familiar to all those New South newcomers.

"In fact," says Sellwyn Crawford, who lives in North Carolina, "it's just the opposite. I think what newcomers are worried about is that the South is losing too much of this kind of thing. It's losing its flavor.

"The new people fit in very well and they take to a lot of our traditions. They learn the rules, but they don't have the eccentricity. I miss that in the New South more than anything. Those wonderful Southern characteristics *and* characters are just becoming homogenized."

There certainly isn't a lot of newcomers in Dallas who resemble Sis Carr. Sis, a civic and philanthropic leader in the city, has always used yellow as her signature color.

Now, this doesn't mean Sis just wears a yellow sweater once in a while. Sis drives a yellow Cadillac, has yellow fingernails and has even dyed her mink coat yellow. Her husband gave her a yellow television set for Valentine's Day. She puts yellow vegetable dye in her grandchildren's milk and has yellow plastic flowers in the yard of her North Dallas estate.

*An original Piggly Wiggly.*

She dyes her Oriental rugs yellow, coats her Boehm porcelain yellow and, of course, has all yellow table linens.

A woman who has recently moved to Dallas was astonished to discover all this yellow when she worked on the same charitable program as Sis.

"Aren't you all surprised at how flamboyant she is?" the newcomer asked another committee member.

"Flamboyant?" she said. "Somehow I've never thought of Sis as flamboyant. She's a lovely grandmother who works tirelessly for this city."

"But what about all that yellow?" the woman wanted to know.

"Oh, that," she said. "That's just Sis."

Courtesy of Piggly Wiggly Corporation, Memphis, Tennessee

## Atlanta, the Mecca

Atlanta *is* the New South. But Old South people from places like Charleston and Savannah say this isn't just something that has occurred in the past twenty-five years with all the influx of new people and new technology.

"Atlanta has always always been nouveau," says a woman from South Carolina. "Even during the war between the states. It never had the history of places like Charleston and Savannah. It was just a little country town. We hear so much about how everything was burned. I believed that lie for a long time. But now I have found out the truth—there wasn't anything there to begin with!"

But no one doubts what's in Atlanta today. Not only is it on the cutting edge of the New South, it's on the cutting edge of what's happening in the world.

The 1996 Summer Olympics will be held in Atlanta. Quite a coup, since such international cities as Athens, Greece, the site of the first Olympics, were also bidding.

The Atlanta committee decided the way to capture the Olympic Games was to bowl over the committee with Southern hospitality. The selection committee was put up in local hotels, but all other entertaining was done in Georgia homes. They spared no detail. If they heard a committee member was a baseball fan, he found himself at dinner sitting next to a famous baseball player. If music was the interest, musicians were in abundance. The committee was even taken to Savannah because the boating part of the Olympics will be held there.

As the buses drove the international visitors through historic Old Savannah, choirs of children were lined up in parks along the way. As the Olympic Committee vehicles passed by, the children serenaded them with renditions of "It's a Small World."

"I talked to one committee member who was so overwhelmed he was beside himself," explains one Atlanta host. "He said he sat next to one woman at dinner who was so charming she could have been Scarlett O'Hara herself. This man was from an Eastern Bloc country and he wasn't used to the elaborate dinner parties we have in places like Atlanta. He didn't speak too much English, either. I'm not sure he didn't think he really *was* sitting next to Scarlett O'Hara. But whatever the case, it worked and we've got the Olympics."

But while most of Atlanta is excited about the 1996 games, there are some who still think in terms of the Old South.

"I'm not so sure I want all those foreigners coming in and messing up our city," explains one. This is not an attitude that's encouraged in *New* Atlanta.

Atlanta is also gaining international fame as the headquarters of Ted Turner's Cable News Network (CNN). Mr. Turner, who many feel is a modern-day Rhett Butler, does not allow any of his correspondents to use the word *foreign* on the air. They must always say *international*. If they slip up, they are fined.

The president of CNN is a Macon, Georgia, native named Tom Johnson who has lived all over the country but is delighted to be back home in the South, a place he

says he has always loved because "Southerners take care of you when you're sick and they come to your funeral."

Where once he would have worked for national networks out of New York or Washington, D.C., Johnson is based in Atlanta but travels the world.

"I was in Moscow in the office of Mikhail Gorbachev the day he signed away Russia," says Johnson. "When the time came for him to sign the document, he didn't have a pen. There was a scramble around the room to find one. I said, 'Mr. Gorbachev, if you would allow me, I would be glad to lend you mine.' He asked if it was an American pen. I said it was a Mont Blanc, probably French or German. He agreed to take it if that was the case. He didn't want to sign away Russia with an American pen."

Johnson notes that after the pen was returned to him, the Smithsonian Institute asked for it, as had Ted Turner.

"But I gave it to my wife, Edwina," says Johnson. "She had given it to me as a gift. I thought that's to whom it should go."

As head of CNN, he is used to getting international phone calls at all hours of the day and night. He particularly remembers one middle-of-the-night call when he was told Ambassador Robert Strauss was calling from Moscow.

"I grabbed a pad and pencil and was prepared to hear anything. But I never could have guessed what came next.

"The ambassador said he and his wife were watching CNN in the American embassy in Moscow and saw an advertisement for some cassette tapes of songs from the fifties that could be ordered through an 800 number. He didn't want to wait the month or so it would take to order them that way. He wanted me to send them immediately."

## Doin' the Delta

In Mississippi, when people talk about the South, they say there is nothing more Southern than the Delta. They explain that traditionally the Delta starts in the lobby of the Peabody Hotel in Memphis and goes to Catfish Row in Vicksburg.

The Delta is a series of small Mississippi towns all along the flat riverbeds of the Mississippi. Parties on the Delta are legendary, and so are the people.

Tennessee Williams grew up in the Delta, as did writer Walker Percy.

"People who don't know," says one former Delta resident, "wonder what on earth there is to do in such a rural area and such small towns. Now I live in Illinois and friends ask me how I could have stood living there. I tell them it was the most wonderful growing up anyone could possibly have. I miss it every day.

"And the people who came from the Delta are astounding. Jim Henson, who invented the Muppets, grew up in Leland. Not all that far away is Rich, the hometown of Tom Harris, who wrote *Silence of the Lambs.*"

One of the most fascinating things about the Delta is how you never know what little gem you're going to run into as you travel from one town to the next.

In Clarksdale, there's the Delta Blues Museum, which is a tribute to native Mississippi blues artists. Blues clubs are all around, and famed musicians from all over the world frequently stop by to give concerts and visit. While there, visitors can stay at the same hotel, in fact in the same room, as the one where blues artist Bessie Smith died.

In Merigold, there's McCarty's pottery shop, which is housed in what Lee McCarty describes as "Uncle Albert's mule barn." Pup and Lee McCarty have had pottery shows all over the world, including Japan.

Visitors stop in to buy the pottery and to listen to the stories of Lee McCarty, who is a never-ending source of gossip and entertainment.

"Do you see that man over there?" he asks, pointing

toward one of the visitors in the shop. "He's from Tupelo and did the flowers for George Bush's inauguration."

Another visitor says she hears some of McCarty's pottery was bought for the Kennedy White House.

"We never discuss our customers," he says, and then starts telling a tale about his wife, Pup.

"When she graduated school," he says, "she did something unthinkable for back then in the forties. She said she wanted to work. Her daddy asked a friend to help her get a job. He said her interests were shopping and reading. They got her a job in the lending library at Kennington's Department Store in Jackson. It was a famous store then, but they sold only one perfume. It was called 'White Shoulders.' For twenty-five years, when you smelled someone wearing 'White Shoulders,' you knew she was from Jackson."

Chester Kossman lives in Marigold and is sales manager of Kossman's, the General Motors car dealership in Cleveland.

His brother, Ed, who's the president of the car company, has lived on the Delta his whole life. He recalls every event that's happened on the Delta over the past forty years by the cars that were driven. A friend was once trying to remember the year a neighbor had died.

"That was in 1956," Kossman remembers. "The family drove to the funeral in their new 1956 Buick Roadmaster."

Kitty Kossman says her brother-in-law, Chester, is typical of Delta

*ZZ Top with statue of Muddy Waters at the Delta Blues Museum.*

residents who hop from one town to another on a moment's notice.

"Chester would go to Memphis (a two-hour drive) for a glass of ice water," she says.

But Chester has a deep love for the Delta. So much so

*The 1993 Dogwood Trail Court in Fairhope, Alabama. (Pictured left to right: Jane Boram, Priscilla Oglesby, Tiffany Elliot, Laura Murphy, Amanda Bell)*

© Richard Scardemalia, Daphne, Alabama

that for most of the charity events in Memphis, he offers to give a guided tour of "A Day in the Delta." This has sold for as high as $1,500.

"I pick them up at the crack of dawn," he says, "and offer champagne. They have their choice of places. There's so much to see and do, you couldn't get it all done in a day. There's the Splash Gambling Casino in Tunica. The American Costume Museum in Ruleville. In Indianola, we stop at Jane Shelton's interior shop to look at her designer fabrics, which she has made in Paris, France. We go to all

*Chester Kossman giving his tour of the Delta. (Pictured left to right: Barbara Huggins, Betsy Speer, host Chester Kossman, Marilyn Newton, Judy Rogers)* © Sarah Huggins

kinds of towns for antiquing, and in Cleveland, there's a dress shop where ladies from Memphis come in to shop."

There's also the Museum of Southern Jewish Culture, the Catfish Museum, the Delta Blues Museum.

"We go home late on this tour," he says. "And once you get past Clarksdale, there's no public place to stop and go to the bathroom until you get to Memphis. But I have good friends in the town of Rich. If we need a bathroom stop, we just knock on their door. They're very gracious and usually provide cocktails and dessert."

# Laid-Back in L.A. (Lower Alabama)

People in Mobile are quick to correct anyone who says that New Orleans is the birthplace of Mardi Gras in the United States. "Mobile had the first Mardi Gras," they say, "*then* it went to Louisiana."

It's a tradition that is highly regarded by Mobilians. Gala parades and partying go on for two weeks. A king and queen are chosen each year, with debutantes and their escorts making up the court.

"The New South is very evident in the balls and parties, but the coronation and the court still go by the old rules."

A woman who designs and makes queen's gowns and trains, as well as those of her court, says that there are some changes in what the queen is wearing these days.

"But they come slowly," she says. "A big change was when we started doing the queen's train puffy one year instead of just flat."

Mobile is surrounded by rivers, bays and, not far away, the Gulf of Mexico. Gulf Shores, Alabama, has become a haven for "snowbirds" from the cold North.

"They call Gulf Shores one of America's best-kept secrets," says Olive Arnett of Toronto, Canada. "The beaches are like sugar. I've been coming here for ten years. It's fantastic."

During the winter months, the rentals in Gulf Shores and surrounding coast towns can be leased by the month. But come April and May, they start renting by the week and the snowbirds go back home.

"But now," says Jimmie Dowdle, a Gulf Shores real estate agent, "they want to stay longer, so they buy their own condos and rent them out to people from the area during the summer months. We get a kick out of that. Now the Southerners are renting from the Yankees."

Chapter Eleven

# Ozark Chic

*I* keep hearing all those jokes on TV about how people in Arkansas are still barefoot hillbillies. Sure there are plenty of people living up in the hills and mountains of Arkansas. Why not? The scenery is breathtaking from their million-dollar houses up in those hills. Those people bought Wal-Mart stock early. They paid *cash* for those homes.

—Little Rock resident on how some people from "up North" view Arkansas

## B lack Tie in Hog Heaven

Bill Clinton's getting elected president of the United States is the biggest thing to happen to Arkansas since the Civil War. Well, at least the biggest thing since the Wal-Mart came.

But this is not without its detractions. Comedians are having a field day with all the Arkansas jokes. They just can't seem to grasp how a state that has a football yell that sounds like a hog call (*Suuuuuuuuuuueeeeeeee*) has produced a man who has the power to declare nuclear war.

But isn't it nice, some Arkansans point out, that the nuclear war phone is red with white accents, just like the colors of the University of Arkansas Razorbacks football team!

Most folks who live in Arkansas, however, are getting a bit touchy and some wear buttons that proclaim, "We live here because we *choose* to live here!"

"If we're such hayseeds," one Southerner maintains, "how did we get two guys from the South in the White House?"

On election night, Arkansans proudly strung banners all over Little Rock declaring, "America, We're Ready."

The real question may be: Is America ready for Arkansas?

John Robinson of the *Boston Globe* said to a Southerner on election night, "What do we call them, *crackers*?" Robinson even suggested that maybe Pamela Harrison of New York City might like to give those Southerners some tips on entertaining. Like a lot of other Easterners, he seemed to think people in the South don't know how to cater anything but a down-home barbecue.

What outsiders need to understand is that people in Arkansas are just kind of laid-back.

Sam Walton, the founder of Wal-Mart, was considered the richest man in America. But until the day he died, he was still living in Bentonville, Arkansas, driving around in his tractor.

Don Tyson, head of Tyson Chicken Company, which employs about 50,000 people, still refers to himself as "a chicken farmer."

But Tyson is a man who likes to have a good time and spares no expense. This goes back a long way. Almost twenty years ago, his daughter wanted a home wedding. But she also wanted a chapel for her ceremony.

Tyson, whose home is in the Ozark mountains, built an entire redwood chapel in his backyard just for the event. The day after the wedding, he tore it down.

It's true people do wear hog-head hats to University of Arkansas football games. But come on, folks. Did you notice that many of the Buffalo Bills fans had painted themselves blue before arriving to cheer on their team at the Super Bowl.

Those same fans who wear hogs' heads also have sky-boxes at the Arkansas football stadium, just like the pro-team fans. The stadium is in the Arkansas mountains and it's quite a slick operation.

Fans also enjoy posh surroundings when the University of Arkansas plays in other parts of the state.

The special section for big-time Razorback fans in Little Rock is called Hog Heaven. Don't let all that folksy carrying on fool you. Folks who own season tickets in Hog Heaven also own custom-made tuxedos.

Little Rock resident Harry Meyers rarely misses a Razorbacks game.

For the big games in Fayetteville, he's somewhat of a legend.

Once, when he was visiting Italy, he saw this giant hog (about five feet tall), kind of an art piece, that had a head that moved up and down. He wasn't sure what people used it for in Italy, but he thought it would make a wonderful conversation piece at the University of Arkansas football games. Meyers had it shipped to Fayetteville.

"We always take the same suite in the same hotel in Fayetteville whenever the team plays a home game," he says. "We store the hog there and put it up in the suite whenever there's a game. It's kind of tradition. People come by and pay their respects, children play with it and others just want their pictures taken with it. Sometimes we put an apple in his mouth."

Meyers is the owner of Meyers Bakery, a Little Rock establishment for eighty years. He's folksy and he yells *suuuuueeee*. His bakery is one of several that supplies English muffins for the McDonald's Egg McMuffin, and that's no small order. His company also helped develop the brown 'n' serve roll.

In fact, he calls his yacht the *Brown 'n' Surf*.

Little Rock is the home of Dillards, the country's largest privately owned department store chain and the home of Stephens, the largest privately owned investment banking firm off of Wall Street.

Admittedly, the city also has a lot of Southern-fried, high-cholesterol food. The night Bill Clinton was elected president, street vendors were hawking fried catfish, fried chicken, fried potatoes and fried funnel cakes.

An out-of-town visitor loved it all, but wondered if her arteries would survive the next four years.

"We're making history here today," a celebrating Arkansan said. "And you just can't make history on five grams of fat a day."

## Could Rotel Dip Be the Pesto of the Nineties?

Max Brantley of the *Arkansas Times* says Rotel Dip is the national appetizer of Arkansas. It's a treat that combines a can of *hot* Rotel tomatoes with generous amounts of melted Velveeta cheese.

"It's everywhere," Mr. Brantley explains. You certainly can't watch an Arkansas football game without Rotel Dip. You can also add sausage or hamburger meat for a real gourmet taste. And don't laugh—in some parts of the world it is considered a gourmet treat.

"I saw some Rotel tomatoes at the very fancy Faucholn in Paris," he says. They were selling for $4.50 a can. At the Wal-Mart you can get three cans for $1.

Brantley thinks it could sure pep up those parties in the White House and that Washingtonians will grow to love it.

"Not that they have to import Velveeta to Washington," he says. "They've had Velveeta in Washington for a long time."

## They're Selling Oscar de la Renta at the Wal-Mart!

"When I lived on the Mississippi Delta, we'd get dressed up on Saturday night and just go to the Wal-Mart and look around," says Terri Casey of Valdosta, Georgia. "Then we'd go out to dinner. Wal-Mart has changed the small-town South. It's changed our lives. It's got everything. Some of their 'super' stores even have places to get your eyeglasses and your hair done, all at the same time. When I was growing up, we were lucky to have a Dairy Queen. Sometimes I just go there to see what they've got in. I couldn't have been more excited if Neiman-Marcus had come to our town."

It's true, there are Wal-Marts in parts of the country other than the South. But somehow Wal-Mart has a Southern soul. Maybe it's because Sam Walton was from Arkansas and just understood small Southern towns.

"The fall fashion show at Wal-Mart in Rockwell, Texas, is a highlight of my year," says Nancy Lenox. "They've got some pretty fancy stuff there. Let me tell you, that place fills up. I mean, they come in all the way from Fate and Royce City."

Ms. Lenox notes she has lots of experience in shopping and can make a comparison.

"I have lived in New York," she says. "I've shopped at Saks and Bloomingdale's. I can get designer perfume and designer clothes at Wal-Mart just like I can in those stores. But I can't get someone in Bloomingdale's to advise me on my brake pads."

In the big towns, Wal-Mart has its more upscale Sam's. It's always a huge warehouse with concrete floors that carries products like laundry detergent in quantities that will keep a small family going for a year.

It also has Mont Blanc pens and such clothing labels as Oscar de la Renta and Perry Ellis.

Women of the New South also buy a lot of their cocktail food at Sam's. They bought so many of Sam's miniature quiches that for a while it appeared that everyone from Natchez to Mobile was using the same caterer (all swearing it was Aunt Lilah's old recipe they stayed up all night making).

Sam's also gives away a lot of free samples. So much that it's become a chic place to lunch.

"When Sam's opened in an upscale area of Dallas," one woman recalls, "it was incredible. They were giving out samples of everything from smoked salmon to prime rib. You couldn't walk two feet without getting another sample.

"You wouldn't believe it, but socialites from all over town were flocking there for lunch. I saw one entire bridge club there. They ate and then went home to play cards."

Some of the people who were coming to this Dallas store got pretty bold. They were used to being served the best of everything in their own homes.

One woman had eaten there free for at least four days in a row. She was getting bolder and bolder and finally got irritated that they were giving away only party food.

"You're going to have to start including some kind of vegetables for us to sample," she told one of the food clerks. "All this rich food with nothing green to balance it just isn't healthy."

## Ten Things in Little Rock That You Won't Find in New York City

1. Ten-cent phone calls.
2. The only diamond mine in the United States just minutes away . . . okay, maybe an hour or so, but who's counting?
3. Sunday brunch at one of the best restaurants in town for under $10.
4. Restaurants where they bring you water with ice without your having to ask.
5. Bars where you won't run into Donald Trump.
6. Cream gravy at the Dairy Queen.
7. Soap containers that read: "Clinton-Gore Cleaning Up America."
8. The Secret Service at the bowling alley.
9. Signs that say "Thank You for Coming."
10. People who mean it.

# A Whiff of Success

Patti Upton has had all the trappings of a true Arkansas belle of the Old South. She was in the Memphis Cotton Carnival, a cheerleader and Miss University of Arkansas. She married a successful man she's crazy about, belongs to the right country clubs and has two great sons.

"But my mother was even more of a belle," she says. "When she was in the Memphis Cotton Carnival, she wore hoop skirts so big that she had to be taken from party to party in a van."

So how does a woman like Patti compete in the New South?

Well, last year the company she heads made $65 million!

As chief executive officer of Aromitique home fragrances, she's Arkansas's most successful woman entrepreneur.

Patti gets touchy when people make fun of Arkansas. She also doesn't like it when people take potshots at her trademark lilac champagne lipstick.

"It's not really lilac, it's pink and it's really a great shade," she says. "I'm a Southern woman and we like to look good. You can wear great clothes and makeup and still be successful."

At fifty-five, Patti has a soft Arkansas drawl and her beauty-queen looks have not deserted her. But this is no fragile flower. She knows her business from top to bottom.

She loves Arkansas. But she's at home in a lot of places. She and her husband have their own jet and can fly door to door from their home in Eden Isle, Arkansas, to Paris, France, in seven hours.

But she's always content to come home to her house in Eden Isle, which has a panoramic view of Greer's Ferry Lake. The house and grounds have been filmed for "Lifestyles of the Rich and Famous."

Patti's life is one of those amazing success stories that

would just seem too improbable if it were a made-for-TV movie.

She founded her home fragrance company by accident ten years ago. At the time, her friend Sandra Horne owned a gift shop. One fall day, Sandra called Patti to help put together a display in the shop to make the store smell seasonal and inviting. Patti used a big bowl and combined scented oil with berries and leaves she'd picked up outside. Customers were impressed. They kept wanting to buy those ingredients. "They said I made everything smell 'just like Christmas.'"

Soon Patti was making these fragrant brews in her kitchen and wondering if she could really make a business out of stuff she found in her backyard. She decided she could and invested $10,000 to start producing "The Smells of Christmas." She named the company Aromatique. She and her husband own 75 percent of the company. Her friend, whose store this all started in, has 25 percent.

The Smells of Christmas line is seasonal, so Patti got to work on other fragrances. From her headquarters in Herber Springs, she now also packages The Smells of Autumn, The Smells of Spring, and bath and body lotions.

Right from the start, Aromatique was getting giant orders from major stores all over the country. Patti was even named to the fragrance board in New York City.

That's where she discovered that no matter how successful she becomes, people are still going to turn up their noses at the mention of Arkansas.

One day she was all dressed up in the lobby of the Pierre Hotel in New York, wearing a designer suit and pearls. A man heard her accent and came over to tell her that she looked so chic he'd have to guess she was from Dallas.

"Arkansas," she said proudly.

"I can't believe it," he told her. He was so shocked, she might as well have told him she was a leper.

"I got the same thing from a man who was sitting next to me at one of our fragrance events. He asked what I did and I told him. He pursed his lips and said he didn't understand how anything creative could possibly come out of that state. He was an old man, so I didn't slug him."

Patti said that at one point she realized she was a success in most places, but still hadn't really conquered

New York. She hired a public relations person to show her the ropes.

"That woman treated me like I was some hick," she says. "She kept telling me how she'd make me known in the Hamptons. She said everything I did was too Arkansas. I briefly got caught up in some of that and even began to eat my food European style (with the knife in the left hand)."

When she got home, her son looked at her like she was crazy.

"'Why are you eating like that?' he wanted to know.

"I told him that that's the way they eat in New York.

"'Well, you're in Arkansas,' he said, 'and it looks silly.'"

Patti says that's when she *really* took a good look at the situation. She was the one with the successful multi-million dollar company. She was also a woman with style and taste. She realized she didn't need to apologize to anyone about anything.

And besides that, the woman in New York gave her a headache. Patti decided the PR woman was going to do things her way from then on.

*Patti Upton—more than just a whiff of success in Arkansas.*

"I went back to New York," Patti recalls, "and watched that woman as she walked into the room where we were meeting. I couldn't believe I was letting her dictate taste to me. There she was in high heels and no stockings. I did what I had to do. I fired her."

# It's Good for What Ails You

There still may be a few sneers about the South in Washington, but there's no doubt that Arkansas is the center of attention.

As soon as Bill Clinton was elected president, the venerable old Willard Hotel announced it would remove all other bottled water from the shelves and serve only Mountain Valley Spring Water, which is bottled in Hot Springs.

But don't think this is just an Arkansas water that's recently become politically correct.

The doctor prescribed low-sodium Mountain Valley Spring Water to President Eisenhower after he had his heart attack. President Nixon took bottles of it to China. President Reagan took bottles to Moscow.

In Hot Springs, the entrance to the spring is behind locked iron gates. It's a state treasure and no one wants to risk its becoming contaminated.

Mountain Valley Spring Water has become quite chic in other parts of the country. In Arkansas, they're a bit more blasé.

"I've heard about it all my life," one Little Rock newspaper columnist wrote. "But I can't say I've ever tasted it. I use the Arkansas stuff that comes from the taps. I'm already paying for that."

## Chapter Twelve

# The Last Word

*N*o matter how many new ways and new rules I've learned traveling to other parts of the country, I still will never forget the things my grandmother always emphasized. My favorite is that you should always wear your neckline lower in the back than you do in the front. It's not the impression you make, it's the impression you leave.

—A Tennessee woman remembering her Old South grandmother

# It's a Whole New World, but We Never Forget Our Roots

Even the oldest of the old guard in the South realize times are changing. But most firmly believe it's those old roots that make even the New South so intriguing and exotic.

But some admit they are sometimes self-conscious of their Southern roots. Particularly the ones who have to do business in the North. That's why David Pence of Greenville, South Carolina, began giving lessons on "How to Control Your Southern Accent" as a night course at Greenville Technical College.

Pence, a speech pathologist, says his students are almost all professional people who get tired of calling people in other parts of the country and having the phone passed around with the Northerners saying "Hey, listen to this" to other colleagues.

"They don't want to lose, abolish or do away with their accents. They just want to control them," he explains.

Four years ago, when he started the class, he had as many as seventeen in his classroom. But right after Bill Clinton was elected, the requests dropped down to almost none. The school temporarily disbanded the class.

Does this mean Southern accents have become a status symbol?

"I'm not saying this will last," says Pence. "I guess it just depends on how well Clinton does."

The University of Mississippi in Oxford is a study in contrasts of the Old and New South. Sorority and fraternity row still looks like a street of old Southern mansions, there is still an annual contest for the best-dressed coed, and the dean of students has had to put out a brochure on how to become a cheerleader because she gets so many requests for this information.

But this is also a serious school with serious students who come from all over the world to study in high-tech classrooms on high-tech subjects. A black woman has been chosen Miss Ole Miss, the campus has a wide range of ethnic diversity and, of course, students still flock to

Oxford to study in the hometown of author William Faulkner.

Ole Miss is also the home of the Center for the Study of Southern Culture, whose director is a soft-spoken Southerner named Bill Ferris.

The center gets calls from all over the world—Africa, Russia, China. Some of them seriously ask Dr. Ferris to please explain "Bubba" to them.

"They find the South exotic," he says. "They also find it familiar. It feels comfortable, not unlike their own worlds, because the South is filled with small towns, family reunions and a kind of attachment to traditions, similar to what people might know in a Russian village or an African community."

There are now thirty graduate students studying at the center, one who chose Ole Miss over Harvard for her graduate degree.

"At Cambridge," she says, "I'd be in a classroom situation. Here I will be living it."

Students who have grown up in other parts of the country are never sure what to expect when they arrive at so Southern a school. They've heard about all the beauty queens and the football team. They also want to know about the politics, the ethnic diversity, the more liberal elements.

"I was very surprised the first day I was on campus," says one graduate student, "to see girls driving by in their cars asking people if they wanted a ride to the polls. These were obviously sorority girls, they had their sorority letters all over their cars."

The newcomer says she was impressed. It wasn't at all what she had expected. She hadn't imagined sorority row would be so active politically. But at all the houses, young women were driving around trying to get people to get out and vote. She had been told sororities were active in the community. Now she believed it.

That night the new graduate student mentioned this to a professor.

"I think that's great," she said. "But I'm a little confused. Was this vote for the senate, the congress, a state office or just a city election? Just what were they voting for today?"

The Oxford professor just smiled.

"Homecoming queen," he answered.

# About the Author

Maryln Schwartz is an award-winning columnist for the *Dallas Morning News* who has appeared in over four hundred newspapers. She is the author of the best-selling *A Southern Belle Primer (Or Why Princess Margaret Will Never Be a Kappa Kappa Gamma)*. A native of Mobile, Alabama, she now lives in Dallas, Texas.